W9-CCJ-088

Understanding

The Catcher in the Rye

New and future titles in the Understanding Great Literature series include:

Understanding *Flowers for Algernon*
Understanding *Hamlet*
Understanding *I Am the Cheese*
Understanding *The Outsiders*
Understanding *Romeo and Juliet*
Understanding *The Yearling*

Understanding

The Catcher in the Rye

UNDERSTANDING GREAT LITERATURE

Stuart A. Kallen

Lucent Books
P.O. Box 289011
San Diego, CA 92198-9011

On cover: J. D. Salinger, author of *The Catcher in the Rye.* July 16, 1951.

Library of Congress Cataloging-in-Publication Data

Kallen, Stuart A., 1955–
Understanding the catcher in the Rye / by Stuart A. Kallen
p. cm. — (Understanding great literature)
Includes bibliographical references and index.
Summary: Discusses the novel, "The Catcher in the Rye," including the life of J. D. Salinger, and the novel's cast of characters and themes.
ISBN 1-56006-783-7
1. Salinger, J. D. (Jerome David), 1919– Catcher in the rye—Juvenile literature. 2. Runaway teenagers in literature—Juvenile literature. 3. Teenage boys in literature—Juvenile literature [1. Salinger, J. D. (Jerome David), 1919– Catcher in the Rye. 2. American literature—History and criticism.] I. Title. II. Series.
PS3537.A426 K35 2001
813'.54—dc21

00-009235

P.O. Box 289011, San Diego, California 92198-9011

Printed in the U.S.A.

Contents

FOREWORD

"Except for a living man, there is nothing more wonderful than a book!" wrote the widely respected nineteenth-century teacher and writer Charles Kingsley. A book, he continued, "is a message to us from human souls we never saw. And yet these [books] arouse us, terrify us, teach us, comfort us, open our hearts to us as brothers." There are many different kinds of books, of course; and Kingsley was referring mainly to those containing literature—novels, plays, short stories, poems, and so on. In particular, he had in mind those works of literature that were and remain widely popular with readers of all ages and from many walks of life.

Such popularity might be based on one or several factors. On the one hand, a book might be read and studied by people in generation after generation because it is a literary classic, with characters and themes of universal relevance and appeal. Homer's epic poems, the *Iliad* and the *Odyssey*, Chaucer's *Canterbury Tales*, Shakespeare's *Hamlet* and *Romeo and Juliet*, and Dickens's *A Christmas Carol* fall into this category. Some popular books, on the other hand, are more controversial. Mark Twain's *Huckleberry Finn* and J. D. Salinger's *The Catcher in the Rye*, for instance, have their legions of devoted fans who see them as great literature; while others view them as less than worthy because of their racial depictions, profanity, or other factors.

Still another category of popular literature includes realistic modern fiction, including novels such as Robert Cormier's *I Am the Cheese* and S. E. Hinton's *The Outsiders*. Their keen social insights and sharp character portrayals have consistently reached out to and captured the imaginations of many teenagers and young adults; and for this reason they are often assigned and studied in schools.

These and other similar works have become the "old standards" of the literary scene. They are the ones that people most often read, discuss, and study; and each has, by virtue of its content, critical success, or just plain longevity, earned the right to be the subject of a book examining its content. (Some, of course, like the *Iliad* and *Hamlet*, have been the subjects of numerous books already; but their literary stature is so lofty that there can never be too many books about them!) For millions of readers and students in one generation after another, each of these works becomes, in a sense, an adventure in appreciation, enjoyment, and learning.

The main purpose of Lucent's Understanding Great Literature series is to aid the reader in that ongoing literary adventure. Each volume in the series focuses on a single literary work that a majority of critics and teachers view as a classic and/or that is widely studied and discussed in schools. A typical volume first tells why the work in question is important. Then follow detailed overviews of the author's life, the work's historical background, its plot, its characters, and its themes. Numerous quotes from the work, as well as by critics and other experts, are interspersed throughout and carefully documented with footnotes for those who wish to pursue further research. Also included is a list of ideas for essays and other student projects relating to the work, an appendix of literary criticisms and analyses by noted scholars, and a comprehensive annotated bibliography.

The great nineteenth-century American poet Henry David Thoreau once quipped: "Read the best books first, or you may not have a chance to read them at all." For those who are reading or about to read the "best books" in the literary canon, the comprehensive, thorough, and thoughtful volumes of the Understanding Great Literature series are indispensable guides and sources of enrichment.

A Little Holden in Everyone

The Catcher in the Rye by J. D. Salinger has been described variously as extremely funny, tragic, uplifting, obscene, and as an American classic. There are very few characters in post–World War II literature who have been as analyzed and discussed as the protagonist of the book, Holden Caulfield. In fact, Holden has spawned what has been labeled the "J. D. Salinger industry" of social and literary critics who have written thousands of pages psychoanalyzing every arcane move of the fictional character.

Although *The Catcher in the Rye* did not achieve "cult" status until the 1960s, Holden Caulfield is very much a product of the late 1940s, a time of conformity when the average high-school boy wore a crew cut, a white shirt and tie, and a sweater vest and the average high school girl wore bobby socks, a pleated skirt, and saddle shoes. Sexual issues were rarely discussed in the open, and anyone uttering a swear word would face suspension from school.

This era of social conformity took place during a time in history when the United States and other democratic countries were challenged by the totalitarian governments of the Soviet Union and China. Fear of Communist infiltration into American society encouraged a Cold War mentality that sought to investigate anyone who challenged traditional values. Senate and congressional anti-Communist hearings in Washington, D.C., focused the government's wrath on hundreds of liberals, socialists, minorities, actors, artists, and others who were suspected of subversion.

Into this milieu strolled the foul-mouthed, insecure Holden Caulfield, an admitted atheist and a troublemaker who questions the forced conformity of American society. Holden peppers his language with words such as *damn, hell, crap,* and *puke*—words considered obscene by the standards of the 1950s. Holden has been thrown out of several schools and does not seem to care. And he is made physically ill by people whom he believes are phony in thought and action. As Douglas T. Miller and Marion Nowak write in *The Fifties: The Way We Really Were,* "In the character of Holden Caulfield, Salinger captured the suffering of every awkward adolescent in a hypocritical, repressive society."[1] And although Holden seems endearingly innocent by today's standards, his speech and attitudes were considered rebellious and obscene in the 1950s and 1960s.

The idea of an alienated teenager was an exciting new concept in 1951, when *The Catcher in the Rye* was first published. The previous generation had grown up in the Great Depression, when unemployment had reached 30 percent, and people rarely rejected the material comforts that were out of reach for many. Holden, on the other hand, wants to run away from his well-to-do parents, prep school, and society and, as he says, build himself a cabin somewhere.

Through the awkward and insecure character of Holden Caulfield, J. D. Salinger tapped into the American psyche and was well rewarded for his efforts. By 1961 *The Catcher in the Rye* had sold over 1.5 million copies worldwide, by 1975 sales numbers reached 9 million, and readers continued to buy 20,000 to 30,000 copies of the book every month well into the 1980s. As of March 2000, *Catcher* had sold over 60 million copies.

Like Holden, Salinger wanted to disappear into the woods somewhere, and so he did. With his millions in book sales, Salinger disappeared from the public eye, moving to rural New Hampshire. And while the reclusive author wrote several more books and short stories, it is Holden Caulfield who is best remembered. For even with his dirty mouth, insecurities, and obvious shortcomings, millions of readers seem to agree that there is a little bit of Holden Caulfield inside everyone. And his rambling monologue that describes three days of his life before Christmas 1950 remains as insightful and amusing today as it has for more than half a century.

CHAPTER ONE

The Life of J. D. Salinger

Holden Caulfield, the central character in *The Catcher in the Rye*, hates phonies. In fact, he hates phony people so much that he grumbles about them on nearly every page of the book that tells his story. After hearing patrons clapping wildly for a piano player showing off in a bar, Holden says that he would hate such adulation. In fact, he would hide from it.

Those words, written by Jerome David Salinger, might just as well have read "piano player, actor, *or writer*" because when Salinger was loudly applauded for writing *The Catcher in the Rye*, he immediately retreated from the public eye and began to live his life as a recluse—as if in a closet.

As *The Catcher in the Rye* grew in popularity in the 1950s, the press and biographers increasingly sought to interview Salinger. And the more he refused their requests, the more his stature as a literary legend grew, even as his output as a writer dwindled to nothing.

Few books have been written about Salinger's life, and he has given very few interviews. After his last story was published in 1965, the reclusive author virtually disappeared from the public eye for more than thirty-five years. But there is little doubt that Salinger's personality was written into Holden Caulfield. John Wenke writes in *J. D. Salinger: A Study of Short Fiction*, "Salinger did state in a 1953 interview with Shirley Blaney, a Windsor, Vermont, high school girl, that his 'boyhood was very much the same as [Holden Caulfield's], and it was a great relief telling people about it.'"[2]

Full of Wit and Humor

Although J. D. Salinger has jealously guarded his privacy, facts about the author's early life have been gathered over the years. Salinger was born on January 1, 1919. His father, Sol Salinger, was the son of a rabbi in Cleveland, Ohio, but Sol left behind the dictates of Judaism to marry a gentile named Marie Jillich, who later changed her name to Miriam. Sol Salinger became a prosperous ham and cheese importer who moved to progressively nicer neighborhoods in New York City's wealthy Upper East Side. In addition to Jerome, the Salingers had a daughter named Doris in 1911, who, like her brother, has refused to give interviews.

J. D. Salinger attended public schools until he was a teenager. According to Warren French in *J. D. Salinger*, Salinger attended New York's McBurney School in 1932, "where he told the interviewer he was interested in dramatics; but he reportedly flunked out after a year."[3] In September 1934 Salinger's father, perhaps hoping to give his son a more disciplined academic career, enrolled him in Valley Forge Military Academy in Pennsylvania. At Valley Forge, Salinger was published for the first time after he wrote a three-stanza poem about the academy that was later set to music and was sung at graduations for years to come.

Salinger edited the school newspaper *Cross Sabers* in his senior year and was in the Glee Club, the Aviation Club, the French Club, and a drama club called the Mask and Spur. He also took an interest in writing at this time and, according to French, "began writing short stories, working by flashlight under his blankets after official 'lights out.'"[4]

It was during this time that Salinger perfected the acerbic writing style that he would use to such great effect in *The Catcher in the Rye*. In the book *In Search of J. D. Salinger*, Ian Hamilton quotes an unnamed classmate of Salinger's at Valley Forge: "[Salinger] was full of wit and humor and sizzling wisecracks. He was a precocious and gifted individual, and I think he realized at that age that he was more gifted with the pen than the rest of us."[5]

"The Skipped Diploma"

The details of Salinger's life in the late 1930s are sketchy. It is known that after his graduation from Valley Forge, he enrolled at Washington Square College at New York University for at least one summer in 1937. In September 1938 Salinger attended Ursinus College, a small institution near Valley Forge Military Academy. While at Ursinus, Salinger wrote a humorous column called "The Skipped Diploma" for the *Ursinus Weekly*. But, after half a semester at college, Salinger quit school. Although he may have been unhappy at Ursinus, he made quite an impression on the women who knew him. One unnamed woman later wrote,

> The "girls" were impressed by Jerry's good looks—tall, dark, and handsome, as we were in awe of his New York City background and worldly ways. Of course, there were other handsome men on campus . . . but Jerry was different—a loner, a critic, and definitely not one of the crowd.[6]

After his short stint at Ursinus, Salinger moved back to New York. In 1939 he enrolled in a short-story writing class at Columbia University. The course was taught by Whitney Burnett, editor of *Story* magazine, a thin periodical that published many novice writers who later went on to great fame, including William Saroyan, Joseph Heller, and, of course, J. D. Salinger. At the time, however, according to French, "Burnett was not at first impressed by the quiet [Salinger], who made no comments and was interested primarily in playwriting; but Salinger's first story, 'The Young Folks' . . . was polished enough to use in *Story*."[7] *Story* was only the first magazine to publish the creative young writer. In 1941 the twenty-two-year-old Salinger saw his stories in print in *Collier's* and *Esquire.*

Salinger continued to live in his parent's apartment on Park Avenue and to write stories that he hoped would someday be published. Having received several rejection letters, Salinger's hopes were raised when one of his stories was accepted by the venerated *New Yorker* magazine. The story, "Slight Rebellion Off Madison," was about a young boy named Holden Caulfield who had run away from a prep school. Salinger's joy turned to bitterness when editors at the *New Yorker* suddenly refused the story. With America rapidly building up its military forces in light of World War II raging in Europe, it was deemed unacceptable to celebrate a boy who was a runaway, a deserter of sorts.

After many rejections, the New Yorker *mag finally accepted one of J. D. Salinger's storie*

The Last Furlough

On December 7, 1941, the Japanese air force bombed the U.S. naval base at Pearl Harbor, Hawaii, and America entered World War II. Salinger was drafted on April 27, 1942, and after basic training, he attended the Officers, First Sergeants, and Instructors School of the Signal Corps. His writing talents were put to use when he was transferred to the Air Service Command in Dayton, Ohio, where he wrote publicity releases.

During this time Salinger continued to submit fiction to national magazines based in New York. *Collier's* published another of Salinger's short stories in December 1942, and the respected *Saturday Evening Post* gave the young author the princely sum of two thousand dollars for a story called "The Varioni Brothers."

In 1943 Salinger was transferred to the Counterintelligence Corps and was sent to Europe. The author continued his success with the *Saturday Evening Post*, and three more of his stories were printed by the magazine. The final one, entitled "The Last Day of the Last Furlough," saw the first published appearance of Holden Caulfield (although in the story he was missing in action). The story is about Holden's brother, Vincent, who is enjoying his last weekend at home before being shipped overseas. The story also closely paralleled Salinger's life at the time.

On June 6, 1944, Salinger and 150,000 other soldiers hit the beaches at Normandy on D day, the first wave of the Allied invasion of France that would eventually help defeat Nazi Germany. Thousands of Americans died that day, but Salinger was with a division that landed five hours after the initial assault. He survived and served in five European campaigns as a special agent in charge of security with the Twelfth Infantry Regiment. During this time, according to Hamilton, the regiment's job in each newly captured town was to locate "communications centers, cut off telephones, and impound the mails. They would then begin interrogating the hundreds of prisoners who were rounded up . . . on the lookout for [Nazi] collaborators and for German army deserters in civilian clothing."[8]

A Serious Creative Writer

Although he was surrounded by war and destruction, Salinger continued his prolific writing. In 1945 he was published in the *Saturday Evening Post, Story, Esquire,* and *Collier's.* In several earlier stories, Holden Caulfield had been mentioned as missing in action, but he appeared at last as a walking, talking character when "Slight Rebellion off Madison" was finally published in the *New Yorker* after a four-year delay.

By late 1945 the respected publishing company Simon and

Schuster made Salinger an offer to publish a collection of his short stories. For reasons unknown, Salinger asked them to wait, and the stories were never published.

At this time, Salinger had become increasingly frustrated trying to turn Holden Caulfield's story into a novel. He had written a ninety-page version of *The Catcher in the Rye* and found an interested publisher, but he became unhappy with the work and began writing a second version.

Meanwhile, Salinger's reputation continued to grow as his short fiction was published by an increasing number of national magazines. The money was good, and Salinger was beginning to develop a reputation as a literary lion in New York. During this period, the author also became interested in Zen Buddhism, an ancient Eastern religion that practices meditation as a means to spiritual enlightenment.

In 1948, after three more of his short stories appeared in the *New Yorker*, Salinger was awarded a contract with the magazine to provide work on a steady basis. According to French, at that time the *New Yorker* was "considered the top of the heap by most young people who aspire to be recognized as serious creative writers."[9] Salinger also continued to write for women's magazines such as *Good Housekeeping* and *Cosmopolitan*. In fact, 1948 turned out to be Salinger's most prolific and creative year.

The pace of Salinger's magazine work, however, slowed in 1949 and 1950, and biographers have guessed that during this time the author was working on *The Catcher in the Rye*.

Catcher Catches On

In the first pages of *The Catcher in the Rye*, Holden Caulfield says that his brother D. B., a talented writer, was prostituting himself in Hollywood by writing for the movies. Caulfield expresses his hatred for movies outright. There is little doubt that Salinger felt the same way about Hollywood. His feelings were derived from an experience he had selling stories to studios.

In 1949 Samuel Goldwyn's studios bought the film rights to Salinger's short story "Uncle Wiggily in Connecticut." The story was rewritten and renamed *My Foolish Heart.* The film, starring Susan Hayward, received an Oscar nomination, but Salinger's brilliant story had been turned into a sentimental tearjerker of a movie that the author could barely recognize as the story he had written. After this experience, Salinger would never again sell the film or television rights to one of his stories.

J. D. Salinger, author of The Catcher in the Rye.

On July 16, 1951, *The Catcher in the Rye* was published by Little, Brown, and Company. At this moment of triumph, the thirty-two-year-old Salinger remained moody and distrustful of the media. According to Wenke, "Salinger . . . found himself at odds with the publisher. He objected to any attempt at publicizing the book or making it available to the press to review, and he insisted that his photograph be removed from the cover."[10] The photo did appear on the back of the book, in spite of Salinger's protests.

Despite the author's misgivings, *The Catcher in the Rye* generally received good reviews and was picked up as the main selection for the Book-of-the-Month Club. In a rare interview, he told a *New Yorker* colleague, "I think writing is a hard life. . . . The compensations are few, but when they come, if they come, they're very beautiful."[11]

The quirky and original *Catcher in the Rye* was different from any other popular novel of the time. It quickly became a best-seller and stayed on the *New York Times* best-seller list for seven months. While most critics praised the book, some were appalled at Holden Caulfield's mixed-up behavior and his excessive use of profanity.

After twenty-nine weeks on the best-seller list, the initial glow of *The Catcher in the Rye* began to fade from the public view. Salinger told the *Saturday Review*,

> The fact is, I feel tremendously relieved that the season for success of *The Catcher in the Rye* is over. I enjoyed a small part of it, but most of it I found hectic and professionally and personally demoralising. Let's say I'm getting good and sick of bumping into that blown-up photograph of my face on the back of the dust-jacket. I look forward to the day when I see it flapping against a lamp-post in a cold, wet Lexington Avenue wind.[12]

Salinger's picture would not bother him much longer—it was removed from the third printing of the book and all subsequent editions.

Moving to a Cabin in the Woods

In March 1953 the paperback edition of *The Catcher in the Rye* was released, and publicity for the book continued unabated. Salinger, hoping to escape from his growing fame, bought a house on a dirt road in Cornish, New Hampshire, where he has lived for the rest of his life. The house, situated on ninety acres of land, had no central heating, no running water, and no electricity. (Another house, which included these amenities, was later built on the property.)

Shortly after the move, Salinger released some of his best short fiction in *Nine Stories*, which rose as high as number nine during its three months on the best-seller list.

During his first year in Cornish, Salinger made friends with some local high-school students. In November he granted an interview to Shirley Blaney. When the interview did not appear on the high-school page of the Claremont, New Hampshire, *Daily Eagle* but instead appeared on the front page, Salinger broke off relations with the students. This interview was the last ever granted by the reclusive author.

Salinger did attend some parties, however, and at a cocktail party in Manchester, New Hampshire, the author met nineteen-year-old London-born Claire Douglas, whom he married in 1955. The couple had three children while Salinger continued to write for the *New Yorker*.

Salinger's subsequent fiction was a narrative series about the Glass family in New York. "Franny" and "Raise High the Roof Beam, Carpenters" were published in 1955. "Zooey" and "Seymore: An Introduction" were published in 1959. When the collection *Franny and Zooey* was published in 1961, it spent six months at the top of the *New York Times* best-seller list. According to French,

> Even though Salinger refused to permit book clubs to circulate the work, it sold more than 125,000 copies within two weeks after its publication. . . . Advertisements needed to consist of nothing but the name of the book and its author. It was a book-seller's dream come true—a work that literally sells itself.[13]

In 1963 the book *"Raise High the Roof Beam, Carpenters" and "Seymour: An Introduction"* was published along with several other *New Yorker* stories. In 1965, *New Yorker* printed the story "Hapworth 16, 1924." It was Salinger's last published work.

Although Salinger remained as elusive as ever, his books were translated into dozens of other languages and were sold all over the world. French writes, "It has even become popular in [Communist] Russia, where possession of a copy of *The Catcher in the Rye* has become a status symbol among discontented adolescents."[14]

Invasion of Privacy

In 1974 a book of Salinger's stories was published without the author's permission. In protest, Salinger called a San Francisco reporter named Lacey Fosburgh and spoke for nearly thirty minutes. He told her, "There is marvelous peace in not publishing. It's peaceful. Still. Publishing is a terrible invasion of my privacy. I like to write. I love to write. But I write for just myself and my own pleasure."[15]

In 1980 *The Catcher in the Rye* surfaced once again when rock star and former member of the Beatles John Lennon was shot to death in New York City. His assassin, Mark David Chapman, was a mentally disturbed young man who was obsessed with *The Catcher in the Rye*. Chapman believed that the former Beatle was the type of phony so hated by Holden Caulfield because Lennon had "sold out" his true beliefs for rock stardom. So twisted was Chapman's logic that after he shot Lennon five times in the back, he sat down on the curb and began to read *The Catcher in the Rye* as he waited for police officers to arrive. In a later interview, Chapman said he heard voices in his head chanting, "The phony must die—says *The Catcher In The Rye!*"[16]

In 1986 author Ian Hamilton attempted to publish *J. D. Salinger: A Writing Life*, an unauthorized biography of the author. Salinger filed a lawsuit claiming copyright infringement because the book quoted unpublished letters he had written. Ironically, the lawsuit probably generated more attention for Salinger than the book would have if it had simply gone to print with no controversy. Salinger was forced to appear in court and to answer personal questions about his future work. When asked what he was working on, the author answered, "Just a work of fiction. That's all. That's the only description I can really give it. . . . It's almost impossible to define. I work with characters, and as they develop, I just go on from there."[17] After fighting the case all the way to the Supreme Court, Salinger prevailed and the book was published as *In Search of J. D. Salinger*, without the disputed letters.

In May 1997 the literary world was abuzz once again with news about J. D. Salinger. Orchises Press announced that it would publish in book form the story "Hapworth 16, 1924"—Salinger's last published work—which had appeared in the *New Yorker* in 1965. It was to be the first new Salinger book in thirty-four years, but after the media began publicizing the event, the book was delayed and never printed.

In 1999 the eighty-year-old reclusive author was once again in the news—this time for love letters he had written in 1972

Mark David Chapman, the man who assassinated John Lennon (pictured), was obsessed with The Catcher in the Rye.

In 1999 Joyce Maynard auctioned Salinger's love letters.

to a Yale undergraduate named Joyce Maynard. At that time, Maynard had written an article for the *New York Times* called "An Eighteen-Year-Old Looks Back on Life." After reading the article, Salinger, who was fifty-three at the time, began writing letters to Maynard telling her they were soul mates. Maynard dropped out of college and moved to Salinger's New Hampshire hideaway.

The relationship lasted less than a year and Maynard respected Salinger's phobic need for privacy until the late 1990s, when she made the decision to auction his letters so that she could pay for her daughter's college tuition. (Maynard had just gone through a divorce and was deeply in debt.) The letters were sold for $156,000 to the founder of a successful computer company and were returned to Salinger. Maynard also wrote a book about her life and her love affair with Salinger called *At Home in the World.*

On January 1, 2000, J. D. Salinger turned eighty-one as the world celebrated the new century. His character, Holden Caulfield, would have been almost fifty. But in the modern world of the twenty-four-hour-a-day news cycle and the non-stop media meddling in the smallest news events, Salinger has successfully guarded his privacy for nearly five decades.

There is little doubt that *The Catcher in the Rye* would be turned into a major motion picture featuring the biggest Hollywood stars if Salinger would only give his permission. Salinger the man will eventually fade away, but Salinger as Holden Caulfield will remain in the public eye for years to come.

CHAPTER TWO

Salinger in Context

The Catcher in the Rye was a best-selling book and later achieved near cult status in the 1950s. The fifties were an era unlike any other in American history. After the end of World War II in 1945, Europe and Japan lay in ruins, destroyed both physically and financially. With the former world powers such as Great Britain, Germany, France, Russia, and Japan struggling for their very survival, the United States emerged as the most powerful and prosperous nation on Earth.

The war had created severe shortages of basic consumer goods in the United States such as clothing, automobiles, and housing. After the war, a large portion of American industry, which had been producing unprecedented numbers of guns, tanks, airplanes, and battleships, quickly took up the manufacture of washing machines, televisions, record players, cars, and other items. A severe postwar housing shortage encouraged the mass construction of suburban housing tracts in farmland surrounding major cities. Coupled with the exponential growth of the new defense industry, which had begun producing jet fighters, nuclear missiles, and battleships to fight the Cold War, unemployment was at record lows, and relatively well-paying jobs were available to all who wanted to work.

The uncertainties during World War II had also caused many couples to postpone marriage and childbearing. When millions of soldiers returned home after the war, most of them got married. As Douglas T. Miller and Marion Nowak write,

> Everyone got married in the fifties, or at least it was a supreme sign of personal health and well-being to be engaged in the social act of marriage and family-raising. . . . In 1955, [an] estimated . . . 92 per cent of all [adult] Americans were or had been married, the highest record in national history.[18]

The unprecedented rush toward marriage, combined with America's growing prosperity, produced what has come to be known as a baby boom. Between 1946 and 1964, 30 million children were born—more than 4 million a year after the mid–1950s. This baby boom formed a huge demographic that influenced everything from the sale of diapers and cars to the popularity of rock and roll. By the late 1950s, millions of these children were reaching their teenage years—and beginning to feel the pains of adolescence expressed so poignantly by Holden Caulfield.

In *The Fifties*, author David Halberstam appraises the decade:

> [The] fifties appear to be an orderly era, one with a minimum of social dissent. Photographs from the period tend to show people who dressed carefully: men in suits, ties, and—when outdoors—hats; women with their hair in modified page-boys, pert and upbeat. Young people seemed, more than anything else, "square" and largely accepting of the given social covenants. At the beginning of the decade, their music was still slow and saccharine, mirroring the generally bland popular taste. In the years following the traumatic experiences of the Depression and World War II, the American dream was to exercise personal freedom not in social and political terms, but rather in economic ones. Eager to be part of the burgeoning middle class, young men and women opted for material well being. . . .

> In that era of general good will and expanding affluence, few Americans doubted the essential goodness of their society.[19]

Halberstam's summation of the 1950s stands in contrast to the attitudes of Holden Caulfield and helps explain why *The Catcher in the Rye* was considered controversial by some.

A Nonconformist

Holden constantly doubts the "essential goodness" of society, and does not accept much that society holds sacred. In a time of growing commitment to traditional religion, Holden says, he is "sort of" an atheist. Holden definitely does not care to become part of the burgeoning middle class. In a decade remembered for its huge, gas-guzzling automobiles, the protagonist in *The Catcher in the Rye* despises that chrome-laden symbol of the American dream.

In fact, Holden's desire to reject society is so strong that he wants to leave New York and run away to live in a primitive cabin in the woods. He tries to convince Sally to run away with him, offering to marry her if she would only share his dream.

Even in affairs of fashion, Holden is a nonconformist. While most boys of his age were wearing dark suits, ties, and traditional gray fedora hats, Holden wears a cheap red hunting hat that he knows looks corny.

Salinger as Holden Caulfield

An aspiring author is often advised by his or her teachers to "write what you know." J. D. Salinger, no doubt, heard this advice in the creative-writing courses he took, and there is little doubt that the author used Holden Caulfield to express what "he knew" about society.

Like Holden, Salinger attended private prep schools. Salinger strongly rejected fame and moved to a primitive cabin in New Hampshire, where he lived out Holden's dream of chopping

Big, expensive cars were just one aspect of society that Holden Caulfield rejected.

wood in the wintertime to feed his woodstove. Salinger, like Holden, was not interested in traditional Western religion and instead studied Zen Buddhism.

Joyce Maynard carried on a correspondence with Salinger in 1972 before having a brief affair with the author (whom she calls Jerry). In her autobiography *At Home in the World*, Maynard describes reading *The Catcher in the Rye* for the first time after exchanging letters with Salinger.

> Although this is my first exposure to [*The Catcher in the Rye*], the voice in the novel is instantly recognizable. It could be Jerry talking. It's not just that Jerry has inserted so many of his opinions—about movies, or books, or actors, or music—into *Catcher in the Rye*. What's familiar is the point of view and the eye of young Holden Caulfield, which is very nearly the same as that of the man with whom I have been corresponding these last few weeks.[20]

Salinger's experiences during World War II influenced his writing.

There was also the matter of the war—a subject Holden Caulfield touches on several times in the book. Salinger was one of the soldiers who had gone ashore at Normandy on D day and for the next several weeks was in the thick of battle as Allied forces took Europe back from the Nazis. During this period, Salinger wrote on his feelings about the war in letters to Whitney Burnett, his editor in New York. Author Paul Alexander describes Salinger's attitudes in the biography *Salinger:*

> For the better part of the month, Salinger had been in a war zone where, as he witnessed mass death and destruction, he knew he, too, could be killed at any moment . . . he simply could not describe the events of the last three or four weeks. What he had witnessed was too horrendous to be put into words.[21]

Author Leila Hadley confirms that the war had caused Salinger great mental distress. When she went on a date with Salinger, she said, "He did talk about the war with me. I gather he had had a nervous breakdown because of the war. He didn't say so specifically, but he certainly hinted at it."[22]

Salinger had a security-sensitive job in the army, and if he did have a nervous breakdown, he probably spoke at length to a psychiatrist, just as Holden Caulfield does throughout *The Catcher in the Rye.*

A Cultural Icon

However closely Holden Caulfield's words express the sentiments of J. D. Salinger, they certainly sum up the attitudes of a growing number of baby boomers who were just beginning to reach their teenage years in the mid-1950s. And as more young people began to identify with the trials and tribulations of Holden, a growing number of social critics realized the importance of *The Catcher in the Rye* and began to explore the themes of the book. According to writer Leerom Medovoi, while *The Catcher in the Rye* was a best-seller in 1951,

> Only in 1957 did literary critics . . . begin to take interest in Salinger's novel. . . . Between 1957 and 1963, critics wrote a vast number of essays about *Catcher* and Salinger's subsequent books. Academic interest then ebbed until, by the sixties, it had slowed to a trickle that it has since remained.[23]

While critical attention may have ebbed by the 1960s, Holden remained a hero to the increasing numbers of antiestablishment hippies who were making headlines across the country. Never before, it seemed, had so many young people criticized the "phony" attitudes of their parents and their government.

Ironically, these alienated white suburban children of the fifties were the best-fed, best-clothed, and best-educated generation in history. They were also the richest. In 1956 *Scholastic* magazine showed that there were 13 million teenagers in the country with a total income of $7 billion a year—a figure 26 percent higher than in 1953. The average teen had a disposable income of about $45 a month—as much money as an entire family of four spent in 1940.

The Paperback Phenomenon

Teenagers spent much of their income on records, entertainment, comic books, and cars. They also increasingly bought paperback books, which were a new form of literature in the marketplace. Before the war, the only books widely available were expensive hardcover editions. By the early fifties, however, changes in book production had revolutionized the publishing business. As author Kenneth Davis writes in *Two-Bit Culture: The Paperbacking of America*,

> Before these inexpensive, widely distributed books came along, only the rarest of books sold more than a hundred thousand copies; a million-seller was a real phenomenon. . . . Overnight the paperback changed that. Suddenly, a book could reach not hundreds or thousands of readers, but millions, many of whom had never owned a book before.[24]

J. D. Salinger was one of the first authors to benefit from this transformation of the publishing business. In 1953, two years after its initial hardcover publication, the rights to *The Catcher in the Rye* were bought by paperback publisher New American Library. The paperback edition of *Catcher* was a huge success, selling more than 250,000 copies a year until 1964. By 1997 more than 80 percent of all sales of the book were paperback editions.

Affluence and Alienation

Possibly the only other product selling faster than paperback books in the 1950s were rock-and-roll records by Elvis Presley, Little Richard, Jerry Lee Lewis, and others. Rock music was invented by African Americans who combined rhythm and blues with more up-tempo country blues. But it was first introduced to white teenagers by a Cleveland disc jockey named Alan Freed in 1951, the same year *The Catcher in the Rye* was published. Freed played records on *The Moondog Show* on a fifty-thousand-clear-watt station whose signal could be picked up by teenagers all over the Midwest. A few years later, Freed moved his show to New York City, and rock-and-roll records began to sell by the millions.

And rock-and-roll music was a way for suburban teenagers to rebel against the conformist attitudes of the 1950s and separate themselves from adult society. As Miller and Nowak explain,

> By mid-decade, rock and roll was fast becoming teenager's music. This big change in musical habit rose out of several historical trends. One of the major factors was the altered state of teenagers themselves. The widespread affluence of the fifties shifted adolescent status. Middle-class white kids were simply expected to go to school and have lots of wholesome spare time. This new standard created a sense of separation [or alienation] among teenagers. . . . In the limbo of transition and luxury, adolescents came to recognize themselves as unique, set apart, different. That perception marked the first throes of the developing postwar youth culture.[25]

This "unique, set apart, different" attitude was perfectly expressed in the character of Holden Caulfield. And just as many teens identified with the sentiments of Elvis Presley when he sang that he was "on lonely street at Heartbreak Hotel," and they also recognized the isolation embodied in the protagonist of *The Catcher in the Rye.*

After the appearance of *The Catcher in the Rye*, the alienated and misunderstood teenage rebel became a popular character in Hollywood movies. The 1952 movie *The Wild One*, starring Marlon Brando, and the 1956 movie *Rebel Without a Cause*, starring James Dean, were based on characters who sneered at authority but, like Holden Caulfield, were really just insecure and lonely boys. Halberstam elaborates in *The Fifties:*

> Marlon Brando and Elvis Presley were only the first of the new rebels from the world of entertainment and art. Soon to come were many others. If there was a common thread, it was that they all projected the image of being misunderstood, more often than not by their parents' generation, if not their own parents themselves.[26]

The Most Banned Book in America

In a 1951 review in *The New York Harold Tribune Book Review* by Virgilia Peterson, Holden Caulfield is described as "contaminated . . . by vulgarity, lust, lies, temptations, recklessness, and cynicism."[27] While the hero of *The Catcher in the Rye* may not have appealed to critics, however, Holden's popularity was not surprising in the context of the 1950s teenage rebellion. And just like rock and roll, Salinger's novel, too, generated great controversies and was banned in some communities.

There was also an element of the risqué in *The Catcher in the Rye* that helped make it popular among high school and college students—and created controversy among social critics. Holden constantly used words like *puke*, *vomit*, and four-letter words that were strictly forbidden in the 1950s. He also reported on sexual situations that were rarely discussed until the late 1960s, including cross-dressing, molestation, and homo-sexuality. In chapter 9 of the novel, Holden is looking out his hotel window and sees a man dressing up in womwn's clothes. Later in the book, when Holden is spending the night at his former teacher's apartment, the man begins to make a pass at him.

Critics attempted to ban *The Catcher in the Rye* for its use of profanity and, according to the MIT Press Bookstore website, because it is "centered around negative activity."[28] Jack Salzman tracks the novel's controversy in *New Essays on "The Catcher in the Rye"*:

> [Censorship] and *The Catcher in the Rye* are almost synonymous. There is no record, as far as I know, that marks

the formal beginning of the censors' attacks on *Catcher*. But the early reviews of the novel that appeared in Catholic World and Christian Science Monitor—reviews that condemned Salinger for recounting "immorality and perversion"—certainly set the tone for the formal censorship that was not far off. In 1960, for example, *Catcher* was removed from the library and the recommend ading list at a high school in San Jose,

Marlon Brando's character in The Wild One *was similar to Holden Caulfield in many ways.*

> California. In Louisville, Kentucky, a teacher who proposed using Salinger's novel in his tenth-grade class was told that he would not be rehired, and the book was dropped from the reading list. And in Tulsa, Oklahoma, a group of parents insisted on the immediate dismissal of a teacher who had assigned what *Time* magazine in its account of the incident called "the most avidly admired novel on modern American campuses." The novel, the parents complained to the school superintendent, had "filth on nearly every page" and was "not fit to read."
>
> In the ensuing years, the attacks on *Catcher* continued unabated, albeit not always successfully. In 1965, the president of a school board in upstate New York declared that *Catcher* was "dirty" and should not be allowed in any secondary school in the country.... In 1972, a Kansas school district's advisory board voted unanimously to recommend that *Catcher* be removed from the district's approved reading list; the school board, however, voted against barring the novel. Not long after, some parents in Massachusetts asked that *Catcher* not be allowed to be taught at a local high school. "It is totally filthy, totally depraved and totally profane," one parent told the school board. "I don't believe a young mind can absorb this book without being scarred." This time, too, the school board refused to ban the novel. But more often the novel has been banned, often enough by 1973 to be mentioned in the American School Board Journal as "the most widely censored book in the U.S."[29]

The Catcher in the Rye continued to generate controversy well into the 1990s. Its use in English classes was challenged in the Corona-Norco, California, school district in 1993, and in New Richmond, Wisconsin, in 1994. The book was also challenged as mandatory reading in Goffstown, New Hampshire, in 1994 according to the MIT Press Bookstore website "because of the vulgar words used and the sexual exploits experienced in the book."[30]

Despite the controversies over the years, to most modern readers, Holden Caulfield seems like an innocent, if slightly confused, young man. He continues to generate compassion and understanding in readers who were born long after young men stopped dressing in suits and ties to go to the movies. But *The Catcher in the Rye* was ahead of its time when it was published, and Salinger explored many topics—sexuality, alienation, and rejection of society's values—that were not in the mass public consciousness until the mid-1960s or later. Because *The Catcher in the Rye* is such a personal story, told in the first person by one character who shares all of his thoughts with the reader, it has a timeless quality. And as a respected piece of literature, *The Catcher in the Rye* will continue to remain an important part of American culture.

CHAPTER THREE

Plot Overview: A Painfully Sensitive Young Man

The Catcher in the Rye is the story of a seventeen-year-old named Holden Caulfield who details the sequence of events that took place in the days before Christmas vacation sometime around the year 1950. As the story begins, Holden reveals that he was a student at Pencey Prep, a prestigious boy's school in Agerstown, Pennsylvania, but he was expelled from the school for flunking his subjects and not applying himself. Holden decides to leave Pencey several days before the end of the term and take the train home to New York City.

Holden leaves the school on Saturday night, believing that the school will not notify his parents of his expulsion until Tuesday or Wednesday. In the meantime, he decides to "rent a room in a cheap hotel in New York and stay until Wednesday.

Holden stays one night in a cheap hotel, but he has some troubles with a prostitute and the elevator operator and so decides to leave. On the second night, after a disastrous visit to the home of a former teacher, he ends up sleeping on a bench in

Grand Central Station. During the day, Holden wanders into several misadventures in New York, calls some old friends for drinks, and even sneaks into his parents' house when they are not home.

Throughout the several days in which the story takes place, Holden reveals his innermost thoughts in a monologue marked by bouts of depression and impulsive and erratic behavior. As the story ends, the reader discovers that Holden is in a mental hospital, or "resting home" as he calls it, and has been telling his story to a psychiatrist the entire time.

Chapter 1: A Crazy Story

As the book opens, Holden Caulfield establishes intimate contact with the reader but refuses to give immediate insight into his upbringing. Instead he says he will speak of the crazy events surrounding last Christmas. He also reveals that at the time of his telling the story he might be in some sort of institution.

Holden reveals that he has already told the story to his brother D. B., who once wrote a terrific book of stories but has since lowered his standards to write movies. Holden begins to describe the Saturday afternoon that was his last day at Pencey Prep, saying that he planned to visit his seventy-year-old history teacher, Mr. Spencer, before he left school for good.

Chapter 2: Having Difficulties

Holden visits Mr. Spencer, who is sick with the grippe, or influenza. The young man becomes depressed as he sees the old sick man. After some friendly conversation, Spencer begins to lecture the boy about having flunked his history class. The teacher reads Holden's poorly composed essay that was written for his history exam. Holden is horrified and claims he won't forgive the man for making Holden suffer through a reading of his own work. Holden reveals to Spencer that Pencey Prep is the third school where he has had some sort of difficulties, and he finally leaves Spencer's home after promising his old teacher that he is just going through a phase and he is going to be all right.

Chapter 3: The Red Hunting Hat

Holden returns to his dorm room in the Ossenburger Memorial Wing, named after an alumnus who made money in the undertaking business. On the way back to his room, Holden talks about his beloved red hunting hat, the kind with a long peak that he wears backwards on his head in defiance of style and good fashion. Holden then gives a short list of his favorite authors (his brother D. B. and Ring Lardner) and his favorite books. Once in his room, the student who lives next door, Robert Ackley, barges in. Holden's appraisal of the pimple-faced neighbor is very harsh and unsympathetic. As Holden tries unsuccessfully to get rid of Robert, Holden's roommate, Ward Stradlater, arrives, announcing that he is in a hurry to meet a girl for a date.

Chapter 4: Jealousy

Holden, who does not have anything special to do, accompanies Ward to the dorm bathroom, and the two converse as Ward shaves. Ward convinces his roommate to write an English composition for him on any subject he wants. Holden agrees, then begins clowning around in the bathroom. Ward reveals that his date is with a girl he just met named Jane Gallagher. Holden is stunned: He knows Jane very well, they were childhood friends, and he harbors romantic feelings for her. After returning to his room Holden obsesses over Stradlater's date with Jane. Robert barges into the room uninvited and the two talk until dinnertime.

Chapter 5: Allie's Death

After dinner, although it is snowing heavily, Holden decides to go into town with Robert and another friend, Mal Brossard, to see a movie. Once they are at the theater, both of Holden's companions discover that they have already seen the movie that is showing, so the boys eat hamburgers and play pinball. They get back to the dorm around a quarter to nine. Mal leaves and Robert stays, talking about sex while picking at his pimples. He finally leaves, and Holden then writes the composition that he promised Ward. Instead of describing rooms or a house, he writes about his brother Allie's baseball glove. Holden reveals that Allie, two years his junior, had contracted leukemia and died several years earlier. The night Allie died, Holden, then thirteen, slept in the garage and punched out all the windows. Holden broke his hand in the process and later his parents sent him to be psychoanalyzed.

Chapter 6: The Roommates Fight

Ward returns to the dorm after his date with Jane Gallagher. He reads the essay that Holden had written for him and complains that it is about a baseball glove, not a room or a house. Holden rips up the essay, throws it away, and begins to question his roommate about his date with Jane. Ward says that he spent the night sitting in a car with her. Holden gets very jealous, asking Ward if the two had sex. When Ward refuses to say, Holden tries to punch him in the mouth. Ward throws Holden to the ground, pins him down, and punches him in the nose.

Chapter 7: Packing His Bags to Leave

Holden goes into Robert Ackley's room and surprises his neighbor with his bloody face. Holden wants to talk, but unsympathetic Robert wants to sleep. Holden turns off the light and Robert begins snoring within minutes. Holden is continually bothered by the image of Ward kissing Jane. Holden decides to run away from Pencey, take the train to New York, and find a cheap hotel where he can stay for a few days. Ward is sleeping as Holden returns to his room, packs his bags, and leaves.

Chapter 8: Conversation on the Train

Holden walks in the cold and snow to the train station, his face still caked with blood from his fight with Ward. Once on the train to New York City, he meets a woman who is the mother of Ernest Morrow, one of his classmates at Pencey. Holden expresses his exceedingly low opinion of Morrow to the reader. Unaware of Holden's dislike of her son, Mrs. Morrow lends Holden a handkerchief and helps him clean the blood off his face.

Chapter 9: Looking into Windows

Holden is lonely when he gets off the train at Penn Station and thinks of several friends whom he could call, but he calls no one. He takes a cab to the Edmont Hotel, checks into a shabby room and stares out the window for a while. He sees a man dressing up in women's clothing in another room. Holden contemplates his love life, declaring several times that he just doesn't understand sex. Although the hour is late, Holden calls Faith Cavendish, a woman whom he does not know, from a phone number given to him by a friend. He invites her to the hotel for drinks, but she turns him down.

Chapter 10: Dancing at the Lavender Room

Holden puts on a clean shirt and decides to go downstairs to the hotel bar, called the Lavender Room. First, however, he contemplates calling his ten-year-old sister, Phoebe, at home. He decides against it, fearing his mother will answer the phone. In the Lavender Room, Holden finds a "putrid" band playing. He sits down at a table next to three thirty-year-old women. Although he refers to the women as "witches," "ugly," and "dopes," he asks them to dance. He dances with them one after another, but the women are tourists and are more interested in watching the people in the bar. Holden sits at their table and buys them many drinks. They leave and he is left alone with a large bill to pay.

Chapter 11: Recalling Days With Jane

Holden sits in the hotel lobby thinking obsessively about Jane Gallagher making love with Ward Stradlater. He talks about how he met Jane and how they once played golf and checkers together. Holden recalls an incident where he and Jane were playing checkers when her alcoholic stepfather, Mr. Cudahy, approached them asking for cigarettes. Jane would not answer her stepfather or look at him, and after he left, the girl began to cry. Holden began kissing her face and hair but not her mouth. Holden asked her if Cudahy had tried to make a move on her, but she said no. After thinking this through, Holden decides to go to a nightclub in Greenwich Village called Ernie's.

Chapter 12: At Ernie's

Holden gets a ride in a "vomity" cab, and asks the driver where the ducks that live in the lagoon in Central Park go in

The interior of New York City's Pennsylvania Station. Not knowing whom to call, Holden leaves the station and goes to a hotel.

the winter. After arguing about it with the driver, Holden asks him into the club for a drink. The driver refuses, and Holden enters the crowded bar. Ernie is playing the piano, and Holden gets a small, cramped table. While Holden makes scathing comments about everyone in the bar, Lillian Simmons, a friend of Holden's brother D. B., approaches him. Holden tells her that D. B. is a writer in Hollywood, and Simmons is very friendly, asking Holden to join her and her date for a drink. Holden refuses, then leaves the bar.

Chapter 13: An Awkward Meeting with a Prostitute

Holden, hoping to save some of his dwindling funds, walks forty-one blocks back to the hotel in the cold New York night. He has no gloves because someone at Pencey stole them, and Holden imagines finding the culprit and punching him in the face. Holden returns to the hotel, saying he felt depressed, even mentioning that he nearly wished he was dead. The elevator operator offers to send a prostitute to Holden's room for five dollars. Holden, depressed and afraid to say no, agrees. He goes back to his room and cleans up. He admits that he is a virgin and begins to get very nervous in anticipation. The prostitute, Sunny, comes into the room and takes off her dress. Holden gives her a fake name and lies about his age. But Holden simply feels depressed, and he asks Sunny if she would just talk to him. After an uncomfortable conversation and no sex, Holden pays Sunny five dollars and she leaves.

Chapter 14: Beaten by the Elevator Man

Holden still cannot sleep and begins thinking about religion. He says he is an atheist, and talks about his dislike for ministers. The elevator operator, Maurice, knocks on Holden's door and comes into the room with Sunny. They demand another five dollars from Holden, who refuses. Maurice beats up Holden while Sunny takes another five dollars out of the young man's

As he walks in the cold New York night, Holden's thoughts turn to assaulting the person who stole his gloves.

wallet. After they leave, Holden lies on the floor for an hour. He takes a bath and attempts to sleep, but he claims he was really contemplating jumping out the window. He says he refrained from this dramatic form of suicide because he didn't want passers-by gawking at his bloody corpse on the sidewalk.

Chapter 15: Calling Sally Hayes

Holden wakes up in the morning and calls an old friend, Sally Hayes, even though he thinks she is "stupid." Holden and Sally had "necked" before, and she is glad to make a date with the young man when he calls. Holden takes his luggage to Grand Central Station and puts it in a locker. While having breakfast in a sandwich bar, he befriends several nuns who are seated nearby. Although he is running out of money, he gives the nuns a ten-dollar contribution and regrets that he could not give them more. After the nuns leave he asserts how money always just makes people more depressed.

Chapter 16: A Record for Phoebe

Holden has two hours to waste until his date with Sally. He decides to buy a rare record called "Little Shirley Beans" for his sister, Phoebe. On the way to the record store he hears a small boy walking down the street singing a song derived from a Robert Burns poem that normally reads,"If a body meet a body coming through the rye." But this boy has replaced the word "meet" with "catch." Holden doesn't know the song, so he accepts the error as correct. Holden buys the record for the high price of five dollars, then he buys tickets to the play *I Know My Love*. He believes Sally will like the play because she appreciates phony stuff like that. Hoping to run into Phoebe, Holden walks through Central Park for a while, then goes to the Museum of Natural History. He does not find her, so he takes a cab to meet Sally.

Chapter 17: A Proposal for Sally

Holden meets Sally, who is dressed nicely and is very happy to see him. On the way to see the play, Holden tells Sally that he loves her, and she says she loves him, too. Holden hates the play, and afterwards, he and Sally go ice-skating at Radio City. Neither of them can skate well, so the couple has soft drinks in a nearby café. Holden is very nervous and begins a long tirade about everything he hates. Sally is taken aback as Holden begs her to run away with him to live in a cabin by a brook. She refuses, and Holden insults her. The date ends badly as Sally leaves, crying.

Chapter 18: Calling Carl Luce

After trying to call Jane Gallagher and receiving no answer, Holden calls an old friend named Carl Luce. They make plans to have a drink later on, and Holden spends a few hours watching a live variety show and a movie at Radio City.

Chapter 19: Drunk and Insulting

Holden meets Luce at the Wicker Bar in the "swanky" Seton Hotel. By the time Luce arrives, Holden is drunk and begins insulting his friend. Relations between the two are hostile. Luce thinks that Holden should see a psychiatrist and leaves as Holden begs him to stay for one more drink.

Chapter 20: Wandering Central Park

Holden stays at the bar and gets extremely drunk until one o'clock in the morning. In this inebriated condition, he calls Sally Hayes. After waking her up, Holden offers to come to her house on Christmas Eve to help trim the tree. She agrees. After he hangs up, he stays in the phone booth trying not to pass out. With nowhere to go and nothing to do, Holden begins to wander Central Park. He drops Phoebe's record and it breaks into dozens of pieces. He walks around the lagoon looking for ducks, and he nearly falls in. Shivering, and with ice in his hair, he counts out his money, discovering that he has

After nearly freezing as he roams through Central Park, Holden finally decides to visit his sister.

only three dollars left. Fearing that he might die of pneumonia, he begins the long walk to his family's apartment.

Chapter 21: Visiting Phoebe

Holden enters his apartment in the dark and walks into the room where Phoebe is sleeping. He turns on a desk lamp and begins to read her school notebooks. Phoebe wakes up, hugs him, and the two talk. She notifies him that their parents are at a party in Norwalk, Connecticut, and will not be home until very late. Phoebe correctly guesses that Holden has been expelled from yet another school, and she repeatedly says that their father will be angry enough to kill him.

Chapter 22: The Catcher in the Rye

Phoebe wants to know why Holden was expelled, and he recites a litany of complaints about Pencey Prep, Robert Ackley, Ward Stradlater, and others. He tells Phoebe about a boy he knew at his previous school, Elkton Hills, named James Castle. James insulted a boy named Phil Stabile, and Phil's friends began beating him. To get away, James jumped out the window and died. After this story, Holden and Phoebe discuss possible careers for Holden, such as a lawyer or doctor. Holden asks Phoebe if she knows the Robert Burns poem that he heard earlier. When Holden mistakenly inserts "catch" into the song phrase, Phoebe points out that the poem actually says, "If a body *meet* a body coming through the rye." Holden dismisses Phoebe's correction and explains that he pictures thousands of little kids playing some big game in a field of rye with no adults or anyone else around except him. Holden says that he imagines himself standing at the edge of a large cliff, and his job is to catch the children if they accidentally start to run over the cliff. He says he knows it's crazy, but all he wants to be is the "catcher in the rye."

Chapter 23: A Dance with Phoebe

Holden calls up a teacher from his previous school, Mr. Antolini, to see if he can stay at his apartment for the night.

Holden respects Antolini because he was the only person who would pick up James Castle after he jumped out of the window. Antolini agrees to let Holden come over. After the phone call, Holden and Phoebe decided to dance to a few songs, then Holden's parents return home. Holden hides in the closet as his mother enters Phoebe's room. Phoebe offers Holden eight dollars she has saved for Christmas presents. Shaken by her kindness, Holden begins to cry and gives her his beloved red hat in return. Finally he sneaks out the front door of the apartment.

Chapter 24: Running from Antolini

Holden walks to Mr. and Mrs. Antolini's apartment on Sutton Place. Antolini is drunk, but the two discuss Holden's expulsion and other matters. Holden again recites the many grievances he had against Pencey Prep. Antolini quotes psychologist Wilhelm Stekel, telling Holden that the mark of the immature man is wanting to die nobly for a cause, while the mark of the mature man is wanting to live humbly for one. Antolini tries to encourage Holden to become a better student because he thinks the young man has great potential. Holden beds down on the couch and falls asleep. He wakes up suddenly to find Antolini caressing his head. Fearing that the teacher is making a pass at him, Holden quickly dresses and leaves the apartment.

Chapter 25: Falling

By this time, it is dawn and Holden has nowhere to go. He takes the subway to Grand Central Station and sleeps on a bench. He is awakened at nine o'clock by crowds of people going to work. Holden wanders down Fifth Avenue, looking at the Christmas trees, decorations, and street-corner Santas. Holden begins to have a breakdown, imagining that when he stepped off a curb, he would simply fall into oblivion and nobody would ever see him again. Then he would make believe he was talking to his dead brother Allie, asking the boy to save

As he wanders down Fifth Avenue looking at the Christmas decorations, Holden begins to have a nervous breakdown.

him. Out of breath and sweating, Holden decides to run away from home and get a job working in a gas station out West. But first he wants to stop by Phoebe's school, say goodbye, and return the money he borrowed from her. Holden enters Phoebe's school, writes a note asking her to meet him at noon at the Metropolitan Museum of Art, and has it delivered by a school employee.

Phoebe arrives wearing Holden's red hunting cap and carrying a suitcase, intending to run away with her brother. He refuses, and Phoebe starts to cry. The two walk to Central Park, where Phoebe rides the carousel. The brother and sister make up, and it starts to rain. Phoebe puts the red cap back on her brother's head and Holden stands in the downpour watching his sister ride the carousel one last time. Overwhelmed by love for his sister, he begins to cry.

Chapter 26: The End of the Story

Holden declares he isn't going to tell any more of his story. He mentions becoming sick and having to talk to a psychologist at the place where he's staying, but he regrets having said so much about his experiences. Finally, Holden says that he misses his old friends Ward and Robert, even Maurice, the elevator operator that beat him up.

CHAPTER FOUR

Cast of Characters

While almost fifty people are mentioned in *The Catcher in the Rye*, Holden Caulfield is the only character intimately portrayed. Holden is the narrator, and the reader is privy to his thoughts, feelings, and desires. All other characters are represented only as Holden perceives them. In *J. D. Salinger: "The Catcher in the Rye,"* Richard Lettis comments on this phenomenon:

> Holden so occupies the center of attention that the other characters do not really emerge from the story. [The] consciousness of [Holden] is the mirror in which we see his environment, and so we are able to see and know people only as [he] sees them. And while Holden is a perceptive and sensitive observer, he is not a novelist; his intention is not to create living beings for us, and his opportunities for viewing and discussing the characters in the story are in most cases limited.[31]

Perhaps the most important people in Holden's life—his parents—are characters who are barely mentioned and are never described. His father never enters the novel, and his mother is only referred to as a voice in Phoebe's dark bedroom.

Holden Caulfield

Holden Caulfield, the protagonist of *The Catcher in the Rye*, is a depressed seventeen-year-old telling the story of his mental breakdown to a psychiatrist in a "rest home" in California. But Holden is also a deep and emotional character, and readers acquire a sense of intimacy with him. Perhaps because, as Lettis writes, "Holden is alive and immediate . . . in the pages of his story, and we can all meet him and judge him through our personal acquaintance."[32]

Because Salinger's hero is so alive and immediate, when *The Catcher in the Rye* was first published, Holden's thoughts and actions created controversy. When the book was banned by the Temple City, California, school board in 1962, Holden's language was described by one parent as

> crude, profane and obscene; not what you would expect of a boy given the advantages of private schools. . . . We protest [Holden Caulfield's] many blasphemies, unpatriotic attitudes, references to prostitution and sexual affairs. [His] continuous slurs [are] down-grading [to] our home life, teaching, profession, religion, and so forth.[33]

These disparaging remarks, commonly used to describe Holden Caulfield, were very serious charges. And the catalog of Holden's sins is long, as described by Lettis:

> As the story opens he has just flunked out of secondary school for the third time, and is about to run away to New York without the knowledge of his parents or the school authorities. While there, he gets drunk (permissible for adults but terrible for a boy), invites a prostitute to his hotel room, tries to pick up girls in a nightclub, insults a girlfriend, tells lies, admits to an interest in sexual perversion, [and] calls himself an atheist.[34]

In addition, Holden describes all of these transgressions in a language rife with words such as *crap, vomit, turd*, and other obscenities. He seems to rejoice in speaking about Robert Ackley's pimples, Selma Thurmer's falsies, Mr. Spencer picking his nose, and further improprieties. This side of Holden Caulfield is clearly not endearing to his many critics.

Defenders of Holden, however, say that he is brave, loyal, sensitive, refreshingly honest, and holds a deep understanding of the good side of human nature in a phony and insensitive world. These contradictions in his character have made Holden Caulfield perhaps one of the most analyzed characters in post–World War II fiction. In fact, after *The Catcher in the Rye* was published, it spawned, according to one critic, a "J. D. Salinger industry," which generated dozens of articles and books that attempted to examine the actions and motives of Holden Caulfield.

Holden is a character caught between the worlds of childhood fantasy and adult responsibility. When he sneaks into his parents' house to visit his sister, Phoebe, he rages against the people he met at Pencey Prep, claiming it was full of "phonies." Throughout the novel it is clear that Holden has little use for adults, who are constantly referred to as phonies.

Children, however, are different. Holden reveals to Phoebe that his dream in life is to stand in a rye field on the edge of a high cliff and stop children who are running through the rye from falling over the edge. To be the catcher in the rye, Holden wants to protect and save innocent children.

Holden's contradictory actions and feelings reveal his adolescent confusion about the world. On one side, he has many adult desires and habits—he chain-smokes, gets extremely drunk, and desires sexual relations with women. On the other side, Holden often speaks of the innocence of children (symbolized in the characters of Phoebe and Allie) and compares this innocence with the phoniness and fakery he sees in his teachers and other adults. This leads Holden to reject the many things adult society embraces, including school, the movies, cars, life in New York, the army, and religion. As Lettis elaborates,

> Why does Holden fail in school? Not because he is lazy or stupid, we may believe, for his intelligence and energy are demonstrable in many parts of the novel. But education is part of maturing, and Holden does not want to grow up lest he become part of the world of phoniness and weakness which he sees all around him. . . . Everywhere we see Holden turning back to the world of childhood for his delight and security. . . . [It] is to Phoebe he turns, not to his parents. He constantly speaks of the memories and activities of childhood, of the pleasure which the company of children can bring. . . . Holden rejects [the] frightening world [of adults] in favor of his brother Allie, who need never grow into that world because he is dead.[35]

Because Holden is pulled toward both childhood and adulthood, his character grows and changes during the three days in which *The Catcher in the Rye* takes place. In *J. D. Salinger*, James E. Miller Jr. writes,

> As the Holden on his journey [through the book] is re-created for us by the Holden on the psychiatrist's couch, we recognize that the journey is more than movement through space—it is a movement, also, from innocence to knowledge, from self-ignorance to self-awareness, from isolation to involvement.[36]

In the end, Holden Caulfield is a sympathetic young man who refuses to accept the phoniness of people as he perceives them, strives for his own vision in an imperfect world, and refuses to compromise with the expectations of the adult world unless he can do so on his own terms.

Holden's Family and Acquaintances

Critic Richard Lettis states that Holden Caulfield is "perceptive and sensitive,"[37] but there are very few characters in *The*

Catcher in the Rye whom Holden portrays in flattering terms. In fact, except for his brothers Allie and D. B. and his sister, Phoebe, Holden dislikes almost everyone else he knows. And it is apparent throughout the novel that Holden really has no friends, only acquaintances.

Robert Ackley

Robert Ackley is a student at Pencey Prep whose dorm room is next door to Holden's. Holden is disgusted by Robert's sinus trouble, pimples, and generally poor hygiene. Despite this, Holden spends time with Robert simply because he is lonely and needs someone to talk to. Even in this capacity, however, Robert fails to live up to Holden's expectation.

Mr. Antolini

Mr. Antolini was Holden's English teacher at Elkton Hills, the school Holden attended before Pencey Prep. According to Holden, Mrs. Antolini was rich, but much older than her husband.

On his second night in New York, Holden visits Phoebe at his parents' apartment. His parents are at a party in Connecticut, but when they return late at night, Holden, with nowhere to stay, flees to Antolini's apartment. Antolini is about the same age as D. B. He was Holden's favorite teacher and, according to English professor Clinton W. Trowbridge, "the nearest thing that Holden knows to the non-phony adult."[38] When James Castle had jumped out the window, it was Antolini who picked him up and carried him to the infirmary.

When Holden arrives at Antolini's apartment, the teacher asks him about flunking out of Pencey. Holden does not feel much like discussing the issue, and Antolini, who is quite drunk, begins to ramble on, lecturing the young man and warning him that he is destined for a horrible fall unless he becomes a better scholar.

Holden finally goes to sleep on the teacher's couch, but he is suddenly awakened when Antolini begins patting his head. Holden, shocked that his teacher is making a sexual advance, begins to yell and quickly exits the apartment, spending the rest of the miserable night sleeping on a bench in Grand Central Station. This is one of the most stunning blows to Holden's mental health. As Trowbridge writes,

> Pursued by doubts about his interpretation of Antolini's apparent homosexuality as well as guilt feelings about his rejection of Antolini ("even if he was a flit [homosexual] he certainly'd been very nice to me"), [Holden] wanders in a state of terrible depression toward literal as well as figurative death.[39]

James Castle

James Castle is a student at Holden's former school, Elkton Hills, who was hounded by bullies until he committed suicide. Holden tells Phoebe that James had refused to take back something he said about a very conceited boy, Phil Stabile. When Phil's six friends tried to make him take it back, James instead jumped out a window and killed himself. Holden was in the shower and missed the event. The imagery here suggests that Holden felt a sense of loss for failing to prevent James's death, to catch him before he fell.

Allie Caulfield

Holden Caulfield's life is most affected by a young boy who is dead at the time of the story: his brother Allie, who died of leukemia on July 18, 1946. He was two years younger than his brother, but, according to Holden, far more intelligent. Allie's teachers were always writing notes to Mrs. Caulfield praising him. Holden was thirteen at the time of his brother's death, but even four years later, at the time of the narrative, Allie's death continues to haunt Holden. As if his life froze at the time of Allie's death, Holden states that he is sixteen but acts like he's thirteen. As critic David Burrows writes, "The death of Allie . . . is seen as the primal event in Holden's life that governs his unconscious, to the extent of tainting all of his adult experience with associations of death."[40]

The death of a loved one so close in age has created a great deal of guilt in Holden. Although he elevated Allie to near sainthood, Holden also felt denied of love by the focus of his parents' attention on his dying brother. He says that his mother never got over the death of her child, and he implies that she was so distraught that she ignored Holden.

Holden, however, had his own way of getting attention—failing school, running away, and even through violent outbursts. The night after Allie's death, Holden slept in the garage and busted out all the windows with his fist. He tried to smash the windows on the car, but his hand was already broken. This emotional eruption caused Holden to be hospitalized and to miss Allie's funeral. According to Edwin Haviland Miller, "[Holden] was unable . . . to witness the completion of the life process, but by injuring himself he received the attention and sympathy which was denied him during Allie's illness."[41]

Allie's death hangs over almost every scene in *The Catcher in the Rye*. And Holden's language is peppered with words such as *dead, crazy, madman, kill,* and *suicide*. He mentions that something or another depresses him almost fifty times in the book. And as Miller writes, "The significance of the repeated phrase 'that killed me' becomes almost self-evident: reflecting his obsession with death, it tells the unsuspecting world that he wishes himself dead, punished, and then reunited with Allie."[42]

D. B. Caulfield

D. B. Caulfield is Holden's older brother who, like a child who has fallen off of a cliff, has fallen from innocence into the phony world of a Hollywood screenwriter. Holden often admires D. B.'s success, talking about his beautiful girlfriend and his Jaguar that cost four thousand dollars. But Holden also criticizes his brother, who was once a "regular writer" but is now, to Holden's dismay, in Hollywood writing for the movies.

Phoebe Caulfield

Phoebe is Holden's ten-year-old sister. In the story, she represents the young Holden and the innocence of childhood for which he yearns. According to Trowbridge, "With Phoebe, Holden is at home in a world of innocence and integrity. He can trust her to take his side, to understand and sympathize."[43] Phoebe, however, knows Holden perhaps better than he knows himself, and she knows her brother has been expelled from school before he tells her. When she asks him why, Holden launches into a tirade about the depressing and phony people at school.

Feeling that he said too many negative things to his sister, Holden confesses to Phoebe his dream to be the catcher in the rye, to redeem himself by saving the children. As Warren French writes in *J. D. Salinger Revisited*, when Holden decides to run away, however, and meets with his sister to repay the money she lent him, "Phoebe arrives for their appointment with her bags packed to challenge his ambition to play catcher in the rye and announces she is going to accompany him on his journey."[44]

Holden deeply regrets that his sister is ready to run away as he has done, and he insists that she stay in school like so many adults have told him to do. Phoebe ends up riding on the Central Park carousel, where Holden is afraid she will fall off the horse as she tries to grab the gold ring. At that point, near the end of the novel, Phoebe forces Holden to abandon his vision as catcher in the rye. He realizes, as with Phoebe, that kids will always grow up and take risks, suffering life's traumas as they mature. Holden's

When Holden watches his sister ride the carousel in the book, he realizes he can't be the catcher in the rye.

tale ends with Phoebe riding the carousel reaching for the gold ring while he stands in the pouring rain.In his final moments of recognizing what he has learned, he claims he is so happy he could cry.

Here, in the final pages of *The Catcher in the Rye*, Holden seems happy to abandon his quest for the elusive gold ring and to leave the aimless quest to the child. The adult Holden stands in the pouring rain, shut out from such childish pursuits.

Jane Gallagher

Jane Gallagher is one of the few females (besides Phoebe) whom Holden actually seems to like. Holden's relationship with Jane is one of childhood innocence, and he says he would rather hold hands with her than have sex with other girls. Holden's innocent vision of Jane is destroyed when he imagines his roommate, Ward Stradlater, having sex with her on a date. Scholar Jonathan Baumbach explains:

> The most memorable love affair Holden has experienced had its fruition in daily checker games with Jane Gallagher, an unhappy, sensitive girl who was his neighbor one summer. She had become the symbol to him of romantic love, that is, innocent love. When Holden discovers that his "sexy" roommate Stradlater has a date with her, he is con-

> cerned not only about the possible loss of Jane's innocence, but about the loss of his dream of her—the loss of their combined checker-playing, love-innocence.[45]

Throughout the novel, Holden's thoughts continue to return to Jane, and he thinks of calling her several times, but does not follow through.

Sally Hayes

Sally Hayes is the only girl in *The Catcher in the Rye* who seems to genuinely like Holden. She invites him to her parents' house to trim the Christmas tree and meets him for a date to see a play. Sally "necks" with Holden in the cab on the way to the show, but Holden thinks she is yet another phony. Holden's unbalanced mental state is demonstrated when he wildly proposes to Sally and suggests that they run off to live in a cabin in New England. Although he is lonely, he acts exceedingly obnoxious around Sally, until she leaves in tears. Holden later calls her late at night and drunkenly apologizes, and Sally forgives him even though he has insulted and hurt her.

Carl Luce

Carl Luce is a student at Whooton who Holden meets for drinks. Even though he is lonely, Holden cannot be civil to Carl, who departs quickly after suggesting Holden seek psychiatric help.

Mr. Spencer

Mr. Spencer was Holden's history teacher at Pencey Prep. After Holden is expelled from school, he goes to see Spencer one last time to say good-bye. Spencer is very old and has the grippe (influenza). Once Holden enters Spencer's room, he regrets his visit because Spencer begins to berate the young man for failing history. Spencer is the first of many adults in *The Catcher in the Rye* who attempt to change Holden's poor attitude and set him on the road to success.

Ward Stradlater

Ward Stradlater is Holden's roommate at Pencey Prep who is everything Holden is not—sexy, popular with women, strong, and good at sports. Ward's qualities make Holden doubt his own, and although Holden criticizes Ward's intellect, it is Holden who has been expelled from school, not his roommate. Ward's sexual relations with Jane Gallagher cause Holden to be depressed and want to puke. The symbolism is explained by Jonathan Baumbach:

> Stradlater spiritually maims Holden. Holden's sole defense, a belief in the possibility of good [Jane Gallagher] in the world, collapses: "I felt so lonesome all of a sudden [Holden says]. I almost wished I was dead."
>
> That Stradlater may have had sexual relations with Jane—the destruction of innocence is an act of irremediable evil in Holden's world—impels Holden to leave Pencey immediately (but not before he quixotically challenges the muscular Stradlater, who in turn bloodies his nose).[46]

Sunny

Sunny is a prostitute who visits Holden's hotel room during an unsuccessful attempt by the young man to lose his virginity.

CHAPTER FIVE

Themes in *The Catcher in the Rye*

Each reader makes his or her own judgments about the meaning and symbolism of a story when reading a novel. Those who read for simple pleasure may never try to draw deep connections between a fictional character and trends in literary scholarship. *The Catcher in the Rye*, however, has been extensively analyzed by critics, psychiatrists, and scholars. Within those hundreds of pages of literary criticism, several major debates emerge such as the aptness of Holden Caulfield's language, the image of Holden as a saint or a psychotic, and the casting of Holden as a modern-day Huckleberry Finn. The insight offered by such analysis stands to offer a deeper and more meaningful understanding of J. D. Salinger's most famous novel.

Holden's Alienation from Society

Salinger, who removed himself from society by becoming a recluse on a rural farm, created one of the more alienated literary characters of the 1950s. Holden Caulfield was nothing if not estranged from the everyday life of the people around him. As the novel opens, Holden is standing on a hill alone, high above the football field where the entire school has assembled for the most important football game of the year.

In fact, he says that the school took football rivalry so seriously that it seems as though the students were expected to kill themselves if the team didn't win.

Holden stands alone while his schoolmates cheer on the team together. Here is his first of many casual references to suicide. This scene sets the stage for the entire novel in which the alienated Holden Caulfield acts as an outside observer and commentator on many basic American traditions considered very important by others, including school, sports, religion, the working world, the military, movies, and so on.

Critic Charles H. Kegel writes about Holden's reaction to phonies:

> [The] main reason for Caulfield's . . . difficulties lies in his absolute hatred of phoniness. And he finds that phoniness, that hypocrisy, not only in the world of his personal contracts, but in the world of art as well. He detests phony books, phony music, phony movies and plays.[47]

Holden is also disaffected from his family. He cannot confide in his parents that he has been expelled from Pencey Prep. Rather than confide in his mother and father, he wanders the streets of New York City with little money and nowhere to go.

Holden's alienation is completed by his nearly total lack of teenage companionship. His peers, whom he describes so disdainfully, are never really friends, only acquaintances. Robert Ackley, his dorm neighbor at Pencey has bad teeth, pimples, and eats like a pig. Holden describes his roommate, Ward Stradlater, as friendly but phony, a conceited slob who shaved with a dirty, rusty razor and thinks of himself as a real hotshot.

In his complete despair after Sally Hayes walks out on their date, Holden invites Carl Luce to meet him for drinks, even though he does not like Carl. Carl agrees, but even in his loneliness, Holden cannot be friendly, and he asks Carl several insulting questions, including whether he's majoring in "Perverts" at Columbia.

Yet Holden's alienation is understandable considering the character faults of his friends. As critic Harrison Smith writes, Holden's friends are

> an unreasonably repulsive lot of lads. . . . His roommate was an arrogant hunter of girls; the boy next door

Holden's alienation from friends and family led him to wander the streets of New York.

> never brushed his teeth and was always picking at his pimples; the group of "intellectuals," the grinds, and the athletes were all phonies to him. But Holden's sense of the phoniness is never contempt. It is worse; it is despair.[48]

In the end, it is this despair, coupled with alienation, that propels Holden towards a nervous breakdown.

The Phony Holden

Holden uses the word *phony* forty-four times in *Catcher*, and it is obvious that the young man is extremely sensitive to phonies—so sensitive, in fact, that he even wants to puke when he hears someone use the word *grand*. Holden loudly complains against those who tell little lies to gloss over harsh realities, those who pose as someone or something they are not, and those who say one thing and then do something else. In Holden's world, practically every adult and almost all of his acquaintances are phonies. The only people who do not lie about their feelings are innocent children—children Holden wants to protect from the evils of adulthood.

What Holden so despises in others, however, he fails to see in himself. As Edward P. J. Corbett writes,

> Holden is himself a phony. He is an inveterate liar; he frequently masquerades as someone he is not; he fulminates against foibles of which he himself is guilty; he frequently vents his spleen about his friends, despite the fact that he seems to be advocating the need for [their] charity.[49]

Most readers sympathize with Holden, however, despite his hypocrisy and phoniness toward others. Holden lets the reader in on the joke, forewarns when he is about to make up a false identity, and justifies his sometimes cruel humor directed at others. It is by this intimacy with the reader that Holden is allowed to judge others by a higher standard than he holds to himself, and to expose the rampant hypocrisy that so many see in modern society.

Holden as the Upper-Class Misfit

Like J. D. Salinger, Holden Caulfield grew up in a world of expensive prep schools, exclusive Park Avenue apartments, and uncommon privilege. Almost all of the adults in his world are professors, lawyers, doctors, and other well-paid and well-respected professionals. His well-to-do peers attend the theater, drink in exclusive bars, and visit museums. There are no poor people in Holden's world, except for a few short-tempered cabdrivers, some working-class girls he meets in a bar, a brutal bellhop, and a prostitute. While he wishes to reject the world of wealthy adults, possibly finding work as a gas station attendant, Holden always seems to realize that when he is going to fall off that proverbial cliff, the true catchers in the rye will be his parents, their money, and their financial ability to send him to expensive schools and psychiatrists.

Christopher Brookeman explains the importance of the prep school as a setting for *The Catcher in the Rye:*

> Salinger locates Holden's story within a very specific social world in which the most significant influence is not some generalized concept of American culture or society, but the codes and practices of a particular instrument of social control—the American prep school. Even when the action moves to New York, Holden stays, in the main, within a finely tuned collegiate culture of dates and moviegoing. This is clear from his description of the sociology of the clientele in a Greenwich Village nightclub named after the resident pianist: "Even though it was so late, old Ernie's was jam-packed, mostly with prep school jerks and college jerks. . . ."

> The evolution of single-sex boarding schools like St. Mark's and Choate (which John F. Kennedy attended) had a specific function which Holden experiences. In its purest form this kind of school was created in the nineteenth century to educate, socialize, and monitor the male offspring of the professional and business classes.... These institutions became places where the young future professionals of the middle and upper classes experienced an extended period of training and socialization.[50]

At the same time, Holden's school friends prove that attending a prep school does little to enhance intelligence, grooming, or honesty. As the story begins, Holden claims no one he knows is very intelligent. Several pages later, Holden laments that someone stole his camel hair coat and says the school is full of crooks.

So while Holden Caulfield was a product of the upper-class American education system, *The Catcher in the Rye* was also an indictment of that system. And just as the protagonist of *The Catcher in the Rye* was a figure of rebellion among young Americans, many of those who propelled Holden to cult hero status were educated college students who could also rebel against the system that would eventually catch them before they fell.

Falling Imagery

Holden Caulfield is the catcher in the rye, and the metaphors of cliffs and falling are used liberally throughout the book. At the beginning of the book, Holden is standing high on a hill while a football game is played below. It is from this peak that he falls as soon as he leaves Pencey Prep. After Ward Stradlater bloodies his face in a dispute over Jane Gallagher, Holden runs from the dorm crying; as he runs downstairs, he notes that someone had littered the stairs with peanut shells and he almost broke his neck by slipping on them.

This is just the beginning in a series of Holden's symbolic and literal downfalls. James E. Miller Jr. elaborates in *J. D. Salinger:*

> On one level, *The Catcher in the Rye* may be read as a story of death and rebirth. . . . Holden is fated, at the critical age of sixteen years, to fall from innocence, to experience the death of the old self and to arise a new Holden to confront the world afresh. . . . The metaphor of the fall is sounded again and again in the closing pages of the novel. Holden himself introduces it, when talking with Phoebe, in his vision of himself as the catcher in the rye. His own stance at the edge of the cliff, is, in fact, precarious; ironically he is unable to prevent his own imminent fall. Mr. Antolini sounds the warning for Holden, directly and fervently, when he tells him that he is heading for "a terrible, terrible fall," and adds: "This fall I think you're riding for—it's a special kind of fall, a horrible kind. The man falling isn't permitted to feel or hear himself hit bottom. He just keeps falling and falling." It is only a short while after this warning that Holden awakens to find Mr. Antolini patting him on the head, abandons in panic this last refuge open to him, and starts to run—or fall—again. The precise motives behind Mr. Antolini's odd, but very human, gesture are obscure, as Holden himself comes shortly to realize: his patting Holden's head is, in its context, certainly a suggestive physical act; but it is also, surely, an act of profound, human, non-sexual affection, a gesture of the spirit as much as of the hand. Mr. Antolini's motives (he has been drinking) are no doubt muddled in his own mind.[51]

After bolting from Antolini's apartment, Holden begins to question his own behavior. Did his former teacher really make a sexual advance, or was he simply drunk and affectionate? Didn't Antolini, after all, pick up James Castle after he committed suicide? And wasn't Antolini kind and considerate to allow Holden to come over at such a late hour? Is Holden becoming a phony, a user of people for his own selfish interests?

After a nearly sleepless night pondering disease and death, Holden once again alludes to falling. He speaks about how every time he stepped off the curb at the end of his block, he felt like he was falling into oblivion. Then, as he starts sweating profusely, Holden makes believe he is asking his little brother, Allie, to help him, begging him not to let Holden disappear into the void.

Suddenly the situation is reversed—instead of Holden catching the child falling off the cliff, he has now himself fallen from innocence, questioning his own, possibly phony, motives concerning Antolini, and suddenly in need of the child to catch him. As Miller writes,

> His sensation of falling is counterbalanced by his fantasy of flight to the Far West where he will become a deaf-mute, cut off from the world in a kind of living death, his innocence desperately preserved. But the real world, the terribly physical world, continues to press in—and down—on him.[52]

At the conclusion of the book, Holden seems to find the strength he needs to rise up, to continue with his life, to go back to school, and to accept things as they are. It seems as though the falling will stop and Holden might possibly become the catcher he dreams of, the catcher of children, such as Phoebe, who might be next to fall.

Holden's Relations with Women

In his adolescent confusion, Holden Caulfield is conflicted over matters of sex and love. Like a young boy in elementary school, he seems to think most girls are gross. Holden describes the working-class women he meets in the Lavender Room as "ugly," "witches," "real morons," and "dopey." When given an opportunity to have sex with Sunny, a prostitute, Holden ultimately refuses—the adult part of him wants to lose his virginity, the child will not let him do it. Although he kissed Jane Gallagher, he most fondly remembers their games of checkers.

On his date with Sally Hayes, Holden refers to her as "phony" and "snobby." In the next breath, however, he is telling her that he loves her and wants to marry her. When she refuses to run off with him, he immaturely insults her and laughs at her tears. As Joyce Maynard writes in *At Home in the World*,

> Holden Caulfield remains a virgin, maintaining that he has had plenty of opportunities to change this. . . . Sex has a significance for him that makes it impossible for him to embark on in a casual way. He has to like the girl a whole lot. But in the end, the only girl he really loves is his little sister.[53]

Holden as Huckleberry Finn

Mark Twain wrote *The Adventures of Huckleberry Finn* in 1884 as a satire about the restrictions and limitations of American society. Huck, like Holden Caulfield, was constantly running into adults who were phony, mean, or downright dangerous. In *Huckleberry Finn*, Twain portrays Huck and his friend, an escaped slave named Jim, traveling down the Mississippi River on a raft, being tossed about by the currents. Holden's uncaring river is symbolized by New York City, where mean, uncaring, and dangerous adults are to be found in hotels, restaurants, and on street corners. Twain, like Salinger, was a master of dialect who used slang and often offensive language to bring his characters to life.

Many similarities can be seen between Holden and Huckleberry Finn, a character created by Mark Twain (pictured).

In 1956 Charles Kaplan was one of the first scholars to point out the similarities between Huck and Holden:

> Each work, to begin with, is a fine comic novel. Each is rich in incident, varied in characterization, and meaningful in its entirety. In each the story is narrated by the central figure, an adolescent whose remarkable language is both a reflection and a criticism of his education, his environment, and his times. Each is fundamentally a story of a quest—an adventure story in the age-old pat-

> tern of a young lad making his way in a not particularly friendly adult world. An outcast, to all intents without family and friends, the protagonist flees the restraints of the civilization which would make him its victim, and journeys through the world in search of what he thinks is freedom—but which we, his adult readers, recognize to be primarily understanding. Society regards him as a rogue, a ne'er-do-well whose career consists of one scrape after another; but the extent to which he is constantly embroiled with authority is exactly the index of his independence, his sometimes pathetic self-reliance, and his freedom of spirit. He is a total realist, with an acute and instinctive register of mind which enables him to penetrate sham and pretense—qualities which, the more he travels through the adult world, the more he sees as most frequently recurring. He has somehow acquired a code of ethics and a standard of value against which he measures mankind—including, mercilessly, himself. There are many people and things—not many, however—that are (in Holden's term) "nice"; there are many more that are "phony." He does not understand the world, but he knows how one should behave in it. The comic irony that gives each novel its characteristic intellectual slant is provided by the judgements of these young realists on the false ideals and romanticized versions of life which they encounter on their travels.[54]

Holden's Inability to Communicate

Holden Caulfield is a masterful observer. Although his language is peppered with crude phrases and slang, his words are sincere and his observations strike with unerring accuracy. Yet while Holden skillfully engages the reader, he seems woefully unable to communicate with the characters who populate his world. As Charles H. Kegel writes, "Throughout the novel, he is troubled with people who are not listening to what he says, who are talking only to be polite, not because they want to communicate ideas."[55]

Holden often mulls over the names of people he would like to call, from his sister, Phoebe, to Jane Gallagher. And while he rarely connects with people he knows, he does manage to call one woman, Faith Cavendish, whom he has never met but whose number he got from a friend at a party. Like most of Holden's other communications, this one ends poorly when the young man's quest for a date is rejected.

Kegel writes about Holden's failed attempts to reach out and speak to someone:

> Holden Caulfield's inability to communicate satisfactorily with others represents itself symbolically in the uncompleted telephone calls and undelivered messages which permeate the novel. Seeing a phone booth is almost more than he can stand, for he almost constantly feels like "giving somebody a buzz." On fifteen separate occasions he gets the urge to communicate by phone, yet only four calls are completed, and those with unfortunate results. Usually the urge dies without his having even attempted to place the call; he seems fearful of what the results will be and rationalizes, "I wasn't in the mood." Likewise, none of the several verbal messages he asks others to deliver for him gets through to the intended receiver; he simply cannot succeed in making contact.
>
> Growing logically out of this prolonged incommunicability is Caulfield's intention to become a deaf-mute. So repulsed is he by the phoniness around him that he despairs of communicating with anybody.[56]

As often happens with people his age, Holden's inability to communicate with phony adults—and even with his own peers—contributes to his rebellious attitude and his apathetic outlook. In Holden's case, it also causes profound isolation and loneliness. After disastrous conversations or phone calls left unmade, Holden's thoughts repeatedly turn to suicide. Ironically, however, it is Holden's excellent ability to clearly communicate his feelings to the reader that has made him such a beloved figure in literature.

Holden's Vulgar Language

If J. D. Salinger had told the story of Holden Caulfield without the many references to sex and bodily functions, the novel probably would not have generated such controversy in the fifties and sixties. (Nor perhaps won such critical praise.) As it is, Holden's use of language caused the book to be banned from coast to coast. In Detroit, according Kegel, "groups like the Detroit Police Department . . . removed the work from Detroit books stalls as 'pornographic trash.'"[57]

Despite his many critics, however, Holden Caulfield uses language in a manner similar to many young men his age—or at least those who grew up in big cities. As author and scholar Donald P. Costello writes, "Most critics who looked at *The Catcher in the Rye* at the time of its publication thought that its language was a true and authentic rendering of teenage colloquial speech."[58]

One hallmark of that vernacular is Holden's repeated use of the phrases, "if you want to know the truth," "it really is," or "I really did." This may be equated with Holden's hatred of phoniness and people who make false statements. When Holden Caulfield says something, he wants to make sure the reader understands that he is not lying, that "it really is true."

As far as Holden's use of profanities, Costello writes,

> Holden's restraints help to characterize him as a sensitive youth who avoids the most strongly forbidden terms, and who never uses vulgarity in a self-conscious or phony way to help him be "one of the boys." Fuck, for example, is never used as a part of Holden's speech.

> The word appears in the novel four times, but only when Holden disapprovingly discusses its wide appearance on walls. The Divine name is used habitually by Holden only in the comparatively weak *for God's sake*, *God*, and *goddam*. The stronger and usually more offensive for *Chrissake* or *Jesus* or *Jesus Christ* are used habitually by Ackley and Stradlater; but Holden uses them only when he feels the need for a strong expression.[59]

As Costello claims, Holden is careful about when and where he uses profane language, but it is this very language that helped make *The Catcher in the Rye* "cool" and subversive in the 1950s and early 1960s. As is often the case with banned books, the debate surrounding the controversy usually pushes the work onto the best-seller lists as the public clamors to see what all the uproar is about. Ironically, without Holden Caulfield's constant stream of *goddams* and *craps*, *The Catcher in the Rye* might not have been read by thousands of teenagers who simply picked up the book because of the forbidden words.

Notes

Introduction: A Little Holden in Everyone

1. Douglas T. Miller and Marion Nowak, *The Fifties: The Way We Really Were*. Garden City, NY: Doubleday, 1975, p. 381.

Chapter 1: The Life of J. D. Salinger

2. John Wenke, *J. D. Salinger: A Study of Short Fiction*. Boston: Twayne, 1991, p. 123.
3. Warren French, *J. D. Salinger*. Boston: Twayne, 1973, p. 22.
4. French, *J. D. Salinger*, pp. 22–23.
5. Quoted in Ian Hamilton, *In Search of J. D. Salinger*. New York: Random House, 1988, p. 23.
6. Quoted in Hamilton, *In Search of J. D. Salinger*, p. 44.
7. French, *J. D. Salinger*, p. 23.
8. Hamilton, *In Search of J. D. Salinger*, p. 85.
9. French, *J. D. Salinger*, p. 27.
10. Wenke, *J. D. Salinger*, p. 126.
11. Quoted in Wenke, *J. D. Salinger*, p. 126.
12. Quoted in Hamilton, *In Search of J. D. Salinger*, pp. 121–22.
13. French, *J. D. Salinger*, p. 32.
14. French, *J. D. Salinger*, p. 31.
15. Quoted in Wenke, *J. D. Salinger*, p. 128.
16. Quoted in WWWBoard, "Articles on Mark David Chapman and Why He Didn't Have a Trail in the Shooting of John Lennon," November 16, 1999. www.chaos.umd.edu/wwwboard/messages/374.html.
17. Quoted in Steven Engel, ed., *Readings on "The Catcher in the Rye."* San Diego: Greenhaven, 1998, p. 20.

Chapter 2: Salinger in Context

18. Miller and Nowak, *The Fifties*, p. 147.
19. David Halberstam, *The Fifties*. New York: Villard Books, 1993, p. x.
20. Joyce Maynard, *At Home in the World*. New York: Picador USA, 1998, p. 88.

21. Paul Alexander, *Salinger.* Los Angeles: Renaissance Books, 1999, p. 96.
22. Quoted in Alexander, *Salinger*, p. 167.
23. Quoted in Joel Forman, ed., *The Other Fifties.* Urbana: University of Illinois Press, 1997, p. 259.
24. Kenneth Davis, *Two-Bit Culture: The Paperbacking of America.* Boston: Houghton Mifflin, 1984, p. xii.
25. Miller and Nowak, *The Fifties*, pp. 291–92.
26. Halberstam, *The Fifties*, p. 479.
27. Quoted in Malcolm M. Marsden, ed., *If You Really Want to Know: A "Catcher" Casebook.* Chicago: Scott, Foresman, 1963, p. 3.
28. MIT Press Bookstore, "Banned Books Month at the MIT Press Bookstore," 1999. mitpress.mit.edu/bookstore/banned.html.
29. Jack Salzman, ed., *New Essays on "The Catcher in the Rye."* Cambridge: Cambridge University Press, 1991, pp. 14–15.
30. MIT Press Bookstore, "Banned Books Month at the MIT Press Bookstore."

Chapter 4: Cast of Characters

31. Richard Lettis, *J. D. Salinger: "The Catcher in the Rye."* Great Neck, NY: Barron's Educational Series, 1964, p. 3.
32. Lettis, *J. D. Salinger*, p. 10.
33. Quoted in Marvin Laser and Norman Fruman, eds., *Studies in J. D. Salinger: Reviews, Essays, and Critiques of "The Catcher in the Rye" and Other Fiction.* New York: Odyssey, 1963, pp. 126–27.
34. Lettis, *J. D. Salinger*, p. 4.
35. Lettis, *J. D. Salinger*, pp. 12–13.
36. James E. Miller Jr., *J. D. Salinger.* Minneapolis: University of Minnesota Press, 1965, p. 12.
37. Lettis, *J. D. Salinger*, p. 3.
38. Quoted in Engel, *Readings on "The Catcher in the Rye,"* p. 45.
39. Quoted in Engel, *Readings on "The Catcher in the Rye,"* p. 46.
40. Quoted in Joel Salzberg, ed., *Critical Essays on Salinger's "The Catcher in the Rye."* Boston: G. K. Hall, 1990, p. 10.
41. Quoted in Harold Bloom, *J. D. Salinger's "The Catcher in the Rye" Bloom's Notes.* Broomall, PA: Chelsea House, 1996, p. 49.

42. Quoted in Bloom, *J. D. Salinger's "The Catcher in the Rye" Bloom's Notes*, p. 50.
43. Quoted in Engel, *Readings on "The Catcher in the Rye,"* p. 44.
44. Warren French, *J. D. Salinger Revisited*. Boston: Twayne, 1988, pp. 43–44.
45. Quoted in Salzberg, *Critical Essays on Salinger's "The Catcher in the Rye,"* p. 59.
46. Quoted in Salzberg, *Critical Essays on Salinger's "The Catcher in the Rye,"* pp. 59–60.

Chapter 5: Themes in *The Catcher in the Rye*

47. Quoted in Laser and Fruman, *Studies in J. D. Salinger*, pp. 54–55.
48. Quoted in Marsden, *If You Really Want to Know*, p. 10.
49. Quoted in Marsden, *If You Really Want to Know*, p. 71.
50. Quoted in Salzman, *New Essays on "The Catcher in the Rye,"* pp. 58–59.
51. Miller, *J. D. Salinger*, pp. 15–16.
52. Miller, *J. D. Salinger*, p. 16.
53. Maynard, *At Home in the World*, p. 88.
54. Quoted in Marsden, *If You Really Want to Know*, p. 127.
55. Quoted in Laser and Fruman, *Studies in J. D. Salinger*, p. 54.
56. Quoted in Laser and Fruman, *Studies in J. D. Salinger*, p. 55.
57. Quoted in Laser and Fruman, *Studies in J. D. Salinger*, p. 53.
58. Quoted in Salzberg, *Critical Essays on Salinger's "The Catcher in the Rye,"* p. 44.
59. Quoted in Salzberg, *Critical Essays on Salinger's "The Catcher in the Rye,"* p. 47.

For Further Exploration

Below are some suggestions for themes or essays that could be written about *The Catcher in the Rye.*

1. Holden Caulfield's roommate, Ward Stradlater, is handsome, strong, and popular with women. His neighbor Robert Ackley is just the opposite, with poor hygiene, bad skin, and an obnoxious personality. Using chapters 3 through 7, examine how Ward and Robert help define Holden by contrast. Compare the descriptions and actions of these two characters to Holden and analyze his attitudes toward them.

2. When Holden runs away from Pencey Prep, he almost falls down the steps of his dormitory when he finally exits. There are many references to falling in *The Catcher in the Rye.* Find them and explain the symbolic connection to Holden's desire to be the catcher in the rye, who prevents children from falling off of a cliff. *See also*: James E. Miller Jr., *J. D. Salinger.*

3. Holden Caulfield curses, lies, and makes withering judgments about most of the characters in the book. Some readers find him offensive, others find him witty and charming. Do you feel that Holden is lovable or repulsive? Why? *See also:* Sanford Pinsker, *"The Catcher in the Rye": Innocence Under Pressure.*

4. Holden first refers to his brother Allie in chapter 5. Although he is dead, Allie is one of the strongest characters in *The Catcher in the Rye.* Find the references to Allie, write a character study of him, and analyze his importance to Holden's actions. *See also:* Steven Engel, ed., *Readings on "The Catcher in the Rye."*

5. Throughout the novel, Holden uses words that shock, exaggerate, and even lie. Is Holden's use of language realistic? Did Salinger need to use such words to tell his story? How does Holden himself feel about certain obscene words? *See also:* Malcolm M. Marsden, ed., *If You Really Want to Know: A "Catcher" Casebook.*

6. Holden is very insulting toward females with whom he is acquainted. Analyze Holden's attitudes toward females, including Phoebe, Jane Gallagher, those whom he meets in the Lavender Room, and Sunny the prostitute. *See also:* Joel Salzberg, ed., *Critical Essays on Salinger's "The Catcher in the Rye."*

7. In chapter 14, Holden refers to religion, saying he cannot pray and feels like an atheist. Later he gives money to some nuns. What is Holden's attitude toward religion? What does he say about preachers and nuns? How do these references help define Holden's character? *See also:* Joel Salzberg, ed., *Critical Essays on Salinger's "The Catcher in the Rye."*

8. Holden often refers with affection to his red hunting hat but gives it to his sister, Phoebe, when she lends him some money. What is the symbolism behind this hat, and why does Holden love it so much? *See also:* Malcolm M. Marsden, ed., *If You Really Want to Know: A "Catcher" Casebook.*

9. It has been said that Holden succeeds in becoming the catcher in the rye when he prevents his sister from running away. How does Phoebe's desire to run away relate to Holden's running and falling? How is it different? *See also:* Richard Lettis, *J. D. Salinger: "The Catcher in the Rye."*

10. A good story must present characters and situations that are believable. How does Salinger make Holden Caulfield realistic? How does he fail? Which characters in *The Catcher in the Rye* are most believable? Do some situations seem unrealistic? What is the general believability of the story? *See also:* Steven Engel, ed., *Readings on "The Catcher in the Rye."*

11. *The Catcher in the Rye* is the story of a young man rebelling against the expectations of a conformist society. What do you think Holden is rebelling against? *See also:* Douglas T. Miller and Marion Nowak, *The Fifties: The Way We Really Were.*

12. *The Catcher in the Rye* has been compared to Mark Twain's novel *The Adventures of Huckleberry Finn.* In what ways does Holden Caulfield compare to Twain's hero? How does Holden's language resemble Huck's? How do the characters in Twain's novel compare to the people who interact with Holden? *See also:* Mark Twain, *The Adventures of Huckleberry Finn*; Malcolm M. Marsden, ed., *If You Really Want to Know: A "Catcher" Casebook.*

Appendix of Criticism

An Idealistic Hero

As has been generally recognized, *The Catcher in the Rye* is the story of a quest, a search for truth in a world that has been dominated by falsity, the search for personal integrity by a hero who constantly falls short of his own ideal, who, in fact, participates in the very falsity he is trying to escape. The dramatic power of the novel stems from two things: that the hero's conflict is both internal and external and that it increases in intensity as his vision of inner and outer falsity becomes more and more overwhelming. What [critic] Leslie Fiedler calls "the pat Happy Ending" is simply the resolution of this conflict, a superbly appropriate one if we take into account what Salinger's intention is.

Thematically speaking, Salinger's intent is to present us with the plight of the idealist in the modern world. The undergraduate's . . . enthusiasm for *The Catcher* shows a recognition of this basic purpose as well as compliments Salinger's rendering of his theme. A college student writes: "Why do I like *The Catcher?* Because it puts forth in a fairly good argument the problems which boys of my age face, and also perhaps the inadequacy with which some of us cope with them. I have great admiration for Caulfield because he didn't compromise. . . . He likes the only things really worth liking, whereas most of us like all the things that aren't worth liking. Because he is sincere he won't settle for less." . . .

What happens to Holden, and what constitutes, therefore, the structural pattern of the novel, is that, as a result of a frighteningly clear vision of the disparity between what is and what ought to be both in the world and in himself and because of an increasing feeling of incapacity to re-form either, he attempts to escape into a series of ideal worlds, fails, and is finally brought to the realization of a higher and more impersonal ideal, that man and the world, in spite of all their imperfections, are to be loved.

Clinton W. Trowbridge, "The Symbolic Structure of *The Catcher in the Rye*," *Sewanee Review*, July–September 1966.

A "Wholly Repellent" Narrative

Mr. Salinger says, "All of my best friends are children. It's almost unbearable to me to realize that my book will be kept on a shelf out of their reach." Many adults as well will not wish to condition themselves to Holden's language. Indeed, one finds it hard to believe that a true lover of children could father this tale. . . .

Holden, who is the clown, villain, and even, moderately, the hero of this tale, is asked not to return to his school after Christmas. This is his third expulsion and he cannot endure to face his parents, so he hides out in New York, where his conduct is a nightmarish medley of loneliness, bravado, and supineness. Jerome David Salinger is an extremely skillful writer, and Holden's dead-pan narrative is quick-moving, absurd, and wholly repellent in its mingled vulgarity, naïveté, and sly perversion.

T. Morris Longstreth, *Christian Science Monitor*, July 1951.

Salinger as Holden Caulfield

Holden goes on to make two points that will no doubt strike those caught up in the Salinger mystique as prophetic of Salinger's own present position with his public. The first is that Holden doesn't think ol' Ernie "knows anymore when he's playing right or not. It's not his fault. I partly blame all those dopes that clap their heads off—they'd foul up anybody, if you gave them a chance." No doubt Salinger has chosen a hermetic life for many complicated reasons, but one suspects that his wish to avoid the adulation that ruined ol' Ernie's art is a major consideration. The other is that Holden, were he a piano player or an actor, would do it quite differently: "I swear to God . . . I wouldn't even want them to clap for me. People always clap for the wrong things. If I were a piano player, I'd play it in the goddam closet." And if Holden were a writer, one imagines him scribbling away in a remote, winterized cabin not unlike that used by . . . Salinger himself in his Cornish, New Hampshire, hideaway.

Sanford Pinsker, *"The Catcher in the Rye": Innocence Under Pressure.* New York: Twayne, 1993.

Ill At Ease in the Modern World

Salinger's most ambitious presentation of aspects of contemporary alienation, and his most successful capture of an American audience, is in his novel *The Catcher in the Rye*. . . . The novel is written as the boy's comment, half-humorous, half-agonizing, concerning his attempt to recapture his identity and his hopes for belonging by playing a man-about-town for a lost, partially tragic, certainly frenetic weekend. [*The Catcher in the Rye's*] dimensional depth is extrinsic to the narrative, and is measured by the reader's response to the dialogue, and the background of city America. It is supplied by one's recognition that Holden Caulfield, sensitive, perceptive, is too aware of the discrepancies between the surface intentions and the submerged motives of himself and of his acquaintances to feel at ease in any world. Through him, Salinger has evoked the reader's consciousness of indefinable rejections and rebellions that are part of the malaise of our times.

Henry Anatole Grunwald, *Salinger: A Critical and Personal Portrait.* New York: Harper & Row, 1962.

The Destruction of Innocence

The most memorable love affair Holden has experienced had its fruition in daily checker games with Jane Gallagher, an unhappy, sensitive girl who was his neighbor one summer. She had become the symbol to him of romantic love, that is, innocent love. When Holden discovers that his "sexy" roommate Stradlater has a date with her, he is concerned not only about the possible loss of Jane's innocence, but about the loss of his dream of her—the loss of their combined checker-playing, love-innocence. Holden has had one previous emotional breakdown at thirteen when his saint-brother, Allie, died of leukemia. In Allie's death, Holden first recognized the fact of evil—of what appears to be the gratuitous malevolence of the universe. Allie, who was, Holden tells us, more intelligent and nicer than anyone else, has become for Holden a kind of saint-ideal. By rejecting an English theme on Allie's baseball glove that Holden has written for him, and by implying that he has "given Jane Gallagher the time," Stradlater spiritually maims Holden. Holden's sole defense, a belief in the possibility of good in the world, collapses: "I felt so lonesome, all of a sudden. I almost wished I was dead."

It is in this state of near-suicidal despair that Holden leaves for New York. That Stradlater may have had sexual relations with Jane—the destruction of innocence is an act of irremediable evil in Holden's world—impels Holden to leave Pencey immediately (but not before he quixotically challenges the muscular Stradlater, who in turn bloodies his nose). At various times in New York, Holden is on the verge of phoning Jane, and actually dials her number twice—that he is unable to reach her is symbolic of his loss of her innocence. The sexually experienced Stradlater, who is [symbolically] one of Holden's destructive fathers in the novel, has destroyed not Jane's innocence so much as Holden's idealized notion of her.

Jonathan Baumbach, "The Saint as a Young Man:
A Reappraisal of *The Catcher in the Rye*,"
Modern Language Quarterly, December 1964.

Ambivalence as a Sign of Mental Instability

Ambivalence is . . . characteristic of Holden and the surest evidence of his mental instability. If he loathes what he loves and does so intensely, he is by no means well. He is also not what he and many readers assume he is: an anti-establishment figure whose disgust is directed entirely at other people. . . . He claims to loathe the perverts he sees through his hotel window but makes a special effort to watch them and even admits that "that kind of junk is fascinating" and that he wouldn't mind doing it himself "if the opportunity came up." He criticizes phony conversations but engages in them himself—with Mr. Spencer and Ernest Morrow's mother, for example. He criticizes "old Spencer" (and others) for using a phony word like "grand," but he himself uses equally phony words such as "nice" and "swell.". . . Obviously, then, Holden is ambivalent, and ambivalence is a certain indication of mental instability.

Duane Edwards, "Holden Caulfield: 'Don't Ever Tell Anybody Anything,'" *English Literary History*, Fall 1977.

An Antireligious Tone

Where condescension serves for pity, the Salinger wit offers savagery as insight, coercing the reader into an attitude out of fear of being stuffy or what is worse, altruistic, reverent, nice. *Catcher in the Rye* subdues a reader summarily in the passages on "old Jesus," who was a "poor bastard," and the Disciples, who "annoy the hell out of" Holden because they did not help "old Jesus." If the reader sympathizes with the passage, the tone disallows him reverence. If he balks at the tone, he is as phony as the Disciples. Should he call off-side against the Christians, no doubt he will be tagged an enemy of free speech.

Robert O. Bowen, "The Salinger Syndrome: Charity Against Whom?" *Ramparts*, May 1962.

Creating Recognizable Teen Speech

In addition to commenting on its authenticity, critics have often remarked—uneasily—[on] the "daring," "obscene," [and] "blasphemous" features of Holden's language. Another commonly noted feature of the book's language has been its comic effect. . . .

Even though Holden's language is authentic teenage speech, recording it was certainly not the major intention of Salinger. He was faced with the artistic task of creating an individual character, not with the linguistic task of reproducing the exact speech of teenagers in general. Yet Holden had to speak a recognizable teenage language, and at the same time had to be identifiable as an individual. This difficult task Salinger achieved by giving Holden an extremely trite and typical teenage speech, overlaid with strong personal idiosyncrasies. There are two major speech habits which are Holden's own, which are endlessly repeated throughout the book, and which are, nevertheless, typical enough of teenage speech so that Holden can be both typical and individual in his use of them. It is certainly common for teenagers to end thoughts with a loosely dangling "and all," just as it is common for them to add an insistent "I really did," "It really was." But Holden uses these phrases to such an overpowering degree that they become a clear part of the flavor of the book; they become, more, a part of Holden himself, and actually help to characterize him.

Donald P. Costello, "The Language of *The Catcher in the Rye*," *American Speech*, October 1959.

Chronology

1919
Jerome David Salinger is born on January 1 in New York City.

1936
Graduates from Valley Forge Military Academy.

1937–1938
Travels to Austria and Poland; attends Ursinus College and New York University.

1939
Enrolls in writing course at Columbia University; World War II begins in Europe.

1940
Publishes first short story, "The Young Folks," in Burnett's literary magazine, *Story*.

1941
The Japanese attack the U.S. naval fleet at Pearl Harbor, prompting the United States to enter World War II.

1942
Salinger serves in the Army Signal Corps and the Counterintelligence Corps.

1944
Lands with American forces on Utah Beach on D day.

1945
World War II ends; Salinger marries a Frenchwoman named Sylvia (maiden name unknown).

1946
Salinger divorces Sylvia.

1950
Senator Joseph McCarthy launches hunt for Communists in the U.S. government; begins what is later called the "Red Scare"; *My Foolish Heart* (film adaptation of "Uncle Wiggily in Connecticut") is released.

1951
The Catcher in the Rye is published in the United States.

1952
Salinger retires to a house in Cornish, New Hampshire.

1953
Nine Stories is published and the book reaches number one on the *New York Times* best-seller list; Salinger gives one of his last published interviews to high school student Shirley Blaney.

1955
Salinger marries Claire Douglas on February 17; a daughter, Margaret Ann, is born December 10.

1960
A son, Matthew, is born; John F. Kennedy is elected president.

1961
The Catcher in the Rye tops 1.5 million in sales.

1965
Salinger's last published work, "Hapworth 16, 1924," is printed in the *New Yorker; The Catcher in the Rye* sales hit 5 million.

1967
Salinger divorces Claire Douglas.

1970
Repays, with interest, advance received from Little, Brown for a book he has yet to write.

1972
The fifty-three-year-old Salinger begins a relationship with eighteen-year-old college student Joyce Maynard.

1974
The unauthorized, pirated collection *The Complete Uncollected Stories of J. D. Salinger* is published; Salinger sues to stop its distribution.

1975
Over 9 million copies of *The Catcher in the Rye* have been sold.

1980
Mark David Chapman assassinates John Lennon in New York City; Chapman is reading *The Catcher in the Rye* when he is arrested minutes later.

1986

Salinger blocks publication of Ian Hamilton's *J. D. Salinger: A Writing Life* due to the inclusion of previously unpublished letters; *The Catcher in the Rye* continues to sell at a rate of twenty to thirty thousand copies a month.

1988

Ian Hamilton publishes *In Search of J. D. Salinger*, without the letters in question.

1996

Salinger's literary agents force "The Holden Server," a *The Catcher in the Rye* website, to shut down because the site randomly generates quotes from the book.

1999

Joyce Maynard publishes, *At Home in the World*, a book about her affair with Salinger in 1972; to raise money to send her daughter to college, Maynard sells love letters written to her by Salinger for $156,000.

Works Consulted

Original Edition of *The Catcher in the Rye*

Jerome David Salinger, *The Catcher in the Rye.* New York: Little, Brown, 1951. The story, according to the dust jacket, of "an ancient child of sixteen, a native New Yorker named Holden Caulfield." This original edition includes material from short stories Salinger wrote about Holden Caulfield in 1945 and 1946.

Other Salinger Works

J. D. Salinger, *Franny and Zooey.* Boston: Little, Brown, 1961. "Franny" was a short story published in the *New Yorker* in 1955 and "Zooey" followed in 1957. Both stories, released in book form in 1961, involve the trials and tribulations of Franny and Zooey Glass.

J. D. Salinger, *Nine Stories.* Boston: Little, Brown, 1953. Nine short stories, such as "A Perfect Day for Bananafish," that were written by Salinger and first appeared in national magazines in the late 1940s.

J. D. Salinger, *"Raise High the Roof Beam, Carpenters" and "Seymour: An Introduction."* Boston: Little, Brown, 1959. Another in the series of short stories about the Glass family that originally appeared on the pages of the *New Yorker.*

About J. D. Salinger

Paul Alexander, *Salinger.* Los Angeles: Renaissance Books, 1999. The latest biography of the reclusive J. D. Salinger. The author is a best-selling biographer who used newly opened archives and personal interviews with more than forty major literary figures to piece together the details of Salinger's life.

Ian Hamilton, *In Search of J. D. Salinger.* New York: Random House, 1988. When Hamilton attempted to publish a biography of Salinger using unauthorized quotes from the author, Salinger went to court to stop the publication. Instead, this book was published by Hamilton without the letters but containing a long section about the court battle and Salinger's part in it.

Joyce Maynard, *At Home in the World.* New York: Picador USA, 1998. In 1972 Joyce Maynard was an eighteen-year-old college student who wrote an illuminating article for the *New York Times.* After reading the article, Salinger, who was fifty-three at the time, began writing letters to Maynard telling her they were soul mates. The two began a short love affair, the details of which Maynard kept secret for twenty-seven years. Maynard's autobiography portrays Salinger in all of his genius and eccentricity.

———, "Joyce Maynard interviews Joyce Maynard," www.joyce maynard.com/works/ahitw-inter.html. This website, maintained by Joyce Maynard, reveals the motives and attitudes behind her decision to break her silence about her 1972 love affair with J. D. Salinger and some of the negative (and positive) public reaction to her revealing autobiography.

Literary Reviews and Criticism

Harold Bloom, *J. D. Salinger's "The Catcher in the Rye" Bloom's Notes.* Broomall, PA: Chelsea House, 1996. This booklet is a short summation of the plot, characters, and symbolism found in *The Catcher in the Rye* by a respected Yale professor and literary critic.

Steven Engel, ed., *Readings on "The Catcher in the Rye."* San Diego: Greenhaven, 1998. A unique anthology that provides accessible resources for students researching J. D. Salinger's most famous work. The essays are taken from a wide variety of sources and are edited to accommodate the comprehension level of young adults.

Warren French, *J. D. Salinger.* Boston: Twayne, 1973. This is the first book-length study of Salinger's work, originally published in 1963. The author, a respected professor of film and literature, explores the themes and structure of Salinger's fiction, including *The Catcher in the Rye* and his later works.

———, *J. D. Salinger Revisited.* Boston: Twayne, 1988. A second volume about J. D. Salinger's work by Warren French. In this book, French compares his early observations with newer and more modern commentaries.

Henry Anatole Grunwald, *Salinger: A Critical and Personal Portrait.* New York: Harper & Row, 1962. Critical analysis of Salinger and his work by such literary heavyweights as John Updike and others.

Marvin Laser and Norman Fruman, eds. *Studies in J. D. Salinger: Reviews, Essays, and Critiques of "The Catcher in the Rye" and Other Fiction.* New York: Odyssey, 1963. A compilation of reviews and critical essays that were written about *Catcher* in the decade after it was published.

Richard Lettis, *J. D. Salinger: "The Catcher in the Rye."* Great Neck, NY: Barron's Educational Series, 1964. A thin volume that acts as a study guide to *The Catcher in the Rye* with insight into the character of Holden Caulfield, questions for study and discussion, and critical comments from other reviewers.

Tim Lieder, "So Where Do the Ducks Go in the Winter?" www.geocities.com/SoHo/Gallery/7466/catcher-rye.html. A website that explores the themes and symbolism behind *The Catcher in the Rye* and provides links to related sites.

Malcolm M. Marsden, ed., *If You Really Want to Know: A "Catcher" Casebook.* Chicago: Scott, Foresman, 1963. A compilation of reviews, literary criticism, and letters to the editor on the subject of J. D. Salinger's famous book.

James E. Miller Jr., *J. D. Salinger.* Minneapolis: University of Minnesota Press, 1965. A short college-level pamphlet that explores the themes and symbolism behind *The Catcher in the Rye,* written by a professor of English at the University of Chicago. This work is part of the University of Minnesota Pamphlets on American Writers series.

Sanford Pinsker, *"The Catcher in the Rye": Innocence Under Pressure.* New York: Twayne, 1993. The author, a professor of humanities at Franklin and Marshall College in Pennsylvania, reflects on *The Catcher in the Rye* and adds a modern perspective to the volumes of critical analysis generated by Salinger's novel.

Joel Salzberg, ed., *Critical Essays on Salinger's "The Catcher in the Rye."* Boston: G. K. Hall, 1990. Another compilation of reviews and literary criticism concerning *The Catcher in the Rye*, this one divided chronologically into reviews from the fifties, sixties, seventies, and eighties. This division helps the reader appreciate Salinger's novel within the changing social context of history.

Jack Salzman, ed., *New Essays on "The Catcher in the Rye."* Cambridge: Cambridge University Press, 1991. A series of critical reviews that evaluate *The Catcher in the Rye* from the perspective of the early 1990s, edited by the Director of the Center for American Cultural Studies at Columbia University.

Harold P. Simonson and Philip E. Hager, *Salinger's "Catcher in the Rye": Clamor vs. Criticism.* Boston: D. C. Heath, 1963. Selected source material for college research papers that pits the negative criticism of *The Catcher in the Rye* against the praise.

John Wenke, *J. D. Salinger: A Study of Short Fiction.* Boston: Twayne, 1991. The first book-length study of Salinger's short fiction, most of which appeared in national magazines in the forties, fifties, and sixties, written by an associate professor of English at Salisbury State University in Maryland.

Historical Background

Kenneth Davis, *Two-Bit Culture: The Paperbacking of America.* Boston: Houghton Mifflin, 1984. A book about the paperback book revolution of the fifties and sixties and its impact on American culture.

Editors of Time-Life Books, *Rock and Roll Generation.* Richmond, VA: Time-Life Books, 1998. An entertaining book full of photos and fascinating facts about teenage life in the 1950s.

Joel Forman, ed., *The Other Fifties.* Urbana: University of Illinois Press, 1997. A series of essays on the 1950s that details the social psychology of the baby boom, the Cold War, the rise of rock and roll, the growth of suburbia, and the tastes of American culture during the postwar decade.

David Halberstam, *The Fifties.* New York: Villard Books, 1993. The definitive eight hundred-page history of the fifties by renowned author David Halberstam. Details the personalities and backgrounds of famous men and women who shaped the fifties.

Douglas T. Miller and Marion Nowak, *The Fifties: The Way We Really Were.* Garden City, NY: Doubleday, 1975. A critical analysis of the 1950s that provides insight into the social mores and cultural events during the era when *The Catcher in the Rye* achieved cult status.

MIT Press Bookstore, "Banned Books Month at the MIT Press Bookstore," 1999. mitpress.mit.edu/bookstore/banned.html. This site, hosted by the Massachusetts Institute of Technology Bookstore, details the attempts by school boards, parents, and others to ban or censor dozens of books, including *The Catcher in the Rye.*

WWWBoard, "Mark David Chapman and Why He Didn't Have a Trail in the Shooting of John Lennon," November 16, 1999. www.chaos.umd.edu/wwwboard/messages/374.html. A website that discusses the motivations of Mark David Chapman, the assassin of former Beatle John Lennon, and his disturbing obsession with Holden Caulfield and *The Catcher in the Rye.*

Index

Picture Credits

Cover Photo: Archive Photos

©AFP/Corbis, 22

Archive Photos, 17

©Yann Arthus-Bertrand/Corbis, 14

©Bettmann/Corbis, 33, 41, 45, 48, 63, 70

©Corbis, 43

©Hulton-Deutsch Collection/Corbis, 27

©Kelly-Mooney Photography/Corbis, 58

©S.I.N./Corbis, 21

©Baldwin H. Ward & Kathryn Ward/Corbis, 28

About the Author

Stuart A. Kallen is the author of over 150 nonfiction books for children and young adults. He has written on topics ranging from the theory of relativity to rock-and-roll history to life on the American frontier. In addition, Mr. Kallen has written award-winning children's videos and television scripts. In his spare time, he is a singer/songwriter/guitarist in San Diego, California.